W0081699

PRAISE FOR *SIKODIWA*

"In a time when we are constantly facing crises, *Sikodiwa* helps us reconnect with our roots and national identity as Filipinos. It offers numerous points for reflection on who we are as a nation, drawing from various perspectives—historical, psychological, and cultural."

—DARWIN RUNGDUIN, RPsy, PhD, associate professor, faculty of
Behavioral and Social Sciences, Philippine Normal University

"For much too long, our understanding of psychological health and healing has been rooted in Western, mechanistic paradigms. These paradigms suit the psychological healthcare of Westernized people, but a vast majority of the world's peoples' conception of a good life and psychological health are rooted in more mystical and mythic conceptions of the human person. In *Sikodiwa*, Cervantes explores Filipino conceptions of the self and being in the world with others and draws from these theories of mental health and therapies of well-being. In this way, he demonstrates how we can broaden counseling practices to be responsive to the people not served by strictly Western psychologies."

—AGUSTIN MARTIN G. RODRIGUEZ, PhD, professor of philosophy,
Ateneo de Manila University

"*Sikodiwa* invites us to pause and rediscover the ancestral wisdom embedded in the Filipino language—wisdom that challenges Western notions of self, society, and success, often rooted in individualism, capitalism, and exploitation."

—CAMILLE ARMAS, program manager for social impact at Canva
Philippines

"Cervantes brings a fresh perspective to the discussion on *Sikolohiyang Pilipino* and well-being in the Philippines. Working in the space of psychosocial support, we have seen his thoughtful work strike deep within the learning space we hold for expressive arts facilitators-in-training. His curiosity has challenged us to ask questions about identity, practice, healing, and our sense of community. Like a colorful and slightly mysterious ancestral home, Carl's work—reflected in this new book—has something for everyone."

—ADRIENNE SANTOS, assistant director at MAGIS Creative Spaces

"Professor Cervantes perfectly captures cultural nuances that many miss. The very term *Filipino* has always been contentious, and he unravels the reasons why by lifting each thread in the tapestry known as the Philippine archipelago. The tension felt by those trying to find themselves amidst a highly globalized world will feel relief after reading this book."

—NIKKI SANTOS-OCAMPO, Philippine creative consultant

"A must-read primer for people and culture-champions committed to fostering safe and inclusive spaces for Filipino talents. This book is both empowering and enlightening, and I highly recommend it to all workplace inclusion allies and advocates."

—CHRISTOPHER M. EUGENIO, board advisor at Philippine Financial
& Inter-Industry Pride

". . . this exploration of Filipino-ness takes you through and beyond the stereotypes, toward and across nuances and forces that shape one another, there and back into distance and time."

—CELINE MURILLO, Filipino nature storyteller

SIKODIWA

SIKODIWA

-

Revisiting Filipino Indigenous Wisdom for Personal and Shared Well-Being

-

Carl Lorenz Cervantes

North Atlantic Books
Huichin, unceded Ohlone land
Berkeley, California

Copyright © 2025 by Carl Lorenz Cervantes. All rights reserved. No portion of this book, except for brief review, may be reproduced, scanned, or distributed in any form or by any means without the written permission of the publisher. No part of this book may be used or reproduced in any manner for the purposes of training artificial intelligence technologies or systems.

North Atlantic Books
Huichin, unceded Ohlone land
2526 Martin Luther King Jr Way
Berkeley, CA 94704 USA
www.northatlanticbooks.com

Cover photo © ilbusca via Getty Images
Cover design by Lauren Smith
Book design by Happenstance Type-O-Rama

Printed in Canada

Sikodiwa: Revisiting Filipino Indigenous Wisdom for Personal and Shared Well-Being is sponsored and published by North Atlantic Books, an educational nonprofit that collaborates with partners to develop cross-cultural perspectives; nurture holistic views of art, science, the humanities, and healing; and seed personal and global transformation by publishing work on the relationship of body, spirit, and nature.

North Atlantic Books's publications are distributed to the US trade and internationally by Penguin Random House Publisher Services. For further information, visit our website at www.northatlanticbooks.com.

The authorized representative in the EU for product safety and compliance is Eucomply OÜ, Pärnu mnt 139b-14, 11317 Tallinn, Estonia, hello@eucompliancepartner.com, +33757690241.

Library of Congress Cataloging-in-Publication Data

Names: Cervantes, Carl Lorenz author
Title: Sikodiwa : revisiting Filipino Indigenous wisdom for personal and
    shared well-being / by Carl Lorenz Cervantes.
Description: Berkeley, CA : North Atlantic Books, 2025. | Includes
    biographical information. | Includes bibliographical references and
    index.
Identifiers: LCCN 2025016596 (print) | LCCN 2025016597 (ebook) | ISBN
    9798889842637 trade paperback | ISBN 9798889842644 ebook
Subjects: LCSH: Filipinos--Psychology | Ethnopsychology--Philippines |
    Philosophy, Philippine | Indigenous peoples--Philippines |
    Philippines--Civilization | Well-being
Classification: LCC BF108.P6 C47 2025 (print) | LCC BF108.P6 (ebook)
LC record available at https://lccn.loc.gov/2025016596
LC ebook record available at https://lccn.loc.gov/2025016597

1 2 3 4 5 6 7 8 9 FRIESENS 30 29 28 27 26 25

Para sa Kapwa
(For Kapwa)

Contents

Contents

Introduction

Tao po! I knock on the door of your inner world, announcing my own humanity *(tao)*, and seeking the humanity within you.

This book is my digestive process, coming from a diet of folk philosophy, indigenous mythology, and humanistic-transpersonal psychology. I offer these thoughts to you; I hope they give clarity and insight, but more importantly, I hope this book calls your spirit homeward. This is a blend of the academic and the personal—it is important that each one should inform the other. It is a cerebral treatise as much as it is a subtle autobiography. As I look inward, I do not see more of myself; rather, I see more of everything else. I share my *pagkatao* (humanness) with everyone else—recognizing this is vital, especially when we must navigate socioeconomic and geopolitical systems that are often hierarchical and individualistic. It is important to disrupt the con that we are separate because alienated and isolated people are much easier to control through fear-mongering and artificial scarcity.

The intuitive recognition of our shared humanity is present in many ancient and indigenous cultures. Through centuries of invasion, oppression, and revolution, these values have persisted, adapting to new containers, assimilating new symbols, appropriating new technology. Culture is invulnerable because it is not only tied to material objects that have been burned and broken, or to stories that have been corrupted or forgotten. Culture is invulnerable because we are alive, and so long as humans continue to interact with their physical and social environments, culture persists. So, as we begin our study, we cannot be distracted by how the spirit chooses to dress up—in modern, Catholic, or even foreign imagery; we must observe how it is *embodied.*

Sikodiwa, from the words *sikolohiya* (psychology) and *diwa* (essence or spirit), is my approach to these mysteries. Drawing wisdom from my own lived experience in Filipino culture, I use the various symbols and customs passed on through generations as gardening tools to cultivate the wisdom within and watch as it blooms. I weed out the parasitic mindsets that have taken root in the ground of my being. I present my inner garden to you, as a contribution to the larger ecosystem of soul gardens. Sikodiwa is not a list of rules about what is and is not; it is a way of thinking and seeing. It is an approach to the world.

Why Read This Book?

Surely you have your own reasons for why you picked this book up— and thank you. I hope you find yourself in it and awaken to the wisdom that has been buried within. This section is for those who are still somewhat unconvinced of its merit and in need of a little nudge. I will imagine myself in the outsider's shoes now, not to preemptively defend my work, but to expound on this book's importance from other angles. I imagine the outsider thinking three questions. First, why should I listen to the ideas of an economically struggling and historically subjugated people? Second, what use are prehistoric beliefs and sociocultural values to the modern world? Third, why should I read something that is specific to an ethnicity that is not my own?

The answer to the first question is ridiculously simple: because we are human too, and our inclusion in the global conversation about human experiences adds realistic nuance to the spectrum of contextual existence. In fact, our historical and economic suffering is a glimpse into what may also await you, should the volatile balance of global power suddenly shift. Understanding the pathways of cultural resilience can help you persist. The dynamics of political and economic power say a lot about human intentions and tendencies; the resistance, subversion, and struggle of oppressed people say a lot about human fortitude, hope, and motivation amidst harsh circumstances; the actions of our ancestors—while colonized or while colonizing others—shape our present identity. A heritage of liberty and strength implies its direct opposite—subjugation and vulnerability—existing somewhere in time. Knowing that we are free implies knowledge of what it is like not to be, either out of historical trauma or out of fear for its near possibility.

The second question is one that has already been answered by many mid-century scholars of the social sciences and humanities. The archetypal processes of human psychology have not changed much, except perhaps that modern people no longer listen to the irrational, mythic symbolism that has, for eons, guided the growth and transformation of great civilizations. Modern people also no longer have clear initiatory rituals, and because of this, many grow up immature and unsure. Whereas, in ancient societies, the transition from child to adult was an awakening of the spirit, today it is just an ubiquitous legal process and a blown-out candle. A return to the prehistoric does not mean regression; it means acknowledging our need to embrace the irrational aspects of our consciousness, in spite of a society that censors our creative primal urges. All that said, I will not actually be talking about prehistoric beliefs at all— everything I will be discussing in the coming chapters are things that I experience today, with many, many, many other people.

Culture is current; the customs and beliefs that still exists today were shaped by years of cultural evolution, as societies adapted to new environmental and human threats. I will bring up historical anecdotes to bring my points across, but they do exist intuitively in the society I live in. I expect that in a hundred years' time, this book may be a relic of thought, and cultural concepts and frameworks may have already transformed— for the better, I hope. Maybe this book can then be a curiosity for the future scholar, in the same way we draw strength and wisdom from the dialogues of ancient history. But even now, as we read those much older manuscripts, we can still be charmed by the fact that a monk in medieval Japan, or a soldier in ancient Rome, or a poet in ancient China, or a dandy in Victorian England, or a prophet in the biblical past can each remind us of our most intimate moments—the taboo lust for what is not ours, the elders' frustration for the increasing waywardness of youth (a complaint we hear in every generation), the pleasant caress of a loved one, or what it feels like to long for home.

The answer to the third question is actually quite similar to the first: because we are human, and we share that sense of being human. Our only difference is that each society emerged from various areas of the planet, influencing our adaptive behaviors. Identification with others, in citizenship or national heritage, is one that is done out of political convenience, but we know two very important things. First, that our place within every society defines our privileges and disadvantages. This means that, even though I share citizenship with millions of other Filipinos, I know that my particular cultural experience is variously defined by my socioeconomic status, gender and sexuality, physical and mental ability, religious affiliation, ethnolinguistic group, access to education, and so on. This means that my experience of Filipino culture may be very different from many others. Citizenship does not guarantee friendship, much to the disappointment of those who seek connections with those who share the same heritage but then begin to see differences in personal identity.

Second, regardless of citizenship, it is possible for me to resonate with anyone sharing my general circumstances. I come from the experience of being Filipino, but I am, first and foremost, human. We can connect deeply regardless of nationality or ethnicity, having been reminded of each other through our shared humanity. In any case, regardless of our differences, many things are undeniably human. Experiences that are totally beyond us are not "inhuman" but rather alternative manifestations of humanness. So, in your reading of this book, if you come across ideas that feel totally alien to you, know that it is true to many others, and if you are open to experiencing it, you may be able to access new and exciting ways of being human.

How to Welcome New Realities

Here is a way to open up, which I also tell my students: A person will only believe in something if they believe it to be true, even if it is, on the surface, incredibly ridiculous. Finding this shared truth gets us closer to understanding our shared humanity. This book is a linear manifestation of my thinking processes, a process that is not itself linear. Other manuals teach in a step-by-step manner, in that learning one concept allows the reader to learn the next, and so on. This is a linear and hierarchical model of learning, where the finished reader becomes unrecognizable to their beginning self. We can try to achieve something similar here, but rather than moving from one chapter to another like steps on a staircase toward the peak, where some idol of absolute truth awaits abandoned, try to think of this book as a philosophical immersion. There is nowhere else to be but where you are. As you read through this book, pay attention to how you react to it; if you like, you can let these ideas seep through your skin and become part of you. Do not expect a massive transformation, wherein you will finally become someone else. Rather, I hope we can set the intention that you should just be who you truly are; a pattern moving through time, shaped like water in the many vessels of body, society, and nature.

Dear Community

For the most part, the work I do is something I do by myself. But my capacity to work, and the distance my work can reach, relies on the trust, encouragement, and feedback of the people around me, as well as the inspiration of people who are no longer with us yet whose voice has been carried through time. I would like to thank, first of all, my editor Jasmine

Respess, for reaching out to me to open up the possibility of a book. It is such an honor to be part of the roster of great authors published by North Atlantic Books. Thank you for believing in my work. I also want to thank my partner, Toni Rose Sarcida, who has been a grounding force throughout my years of seeking, discourse, immersion, and madness. Without her, I would be flying with nowhere to go, and, like the tragic Icarus, I would likely melt my own wax wings and fall. Since this work is also inspired by my personal experiences, I would like to honor my parents—my mother, whose faith and magic has kept me dreaming; and my father, whose steady pragmatism has kept me going. I extend my gratitude to family and friends, as well as those who have been following my work. I know who I am through you, my *kapwa,* my beloved other, with whom I share my humanity.

My work is guided in this direction thanks to the efforts that have been done by my scholarly predecessors in the local social sciences. I am grateful to my academic mentors, who have already opened the intellectual doors through which I enter. This is an adventure for me, having been given the opportunity to participate in this great tradition. As to my spiritual mentors—Father Jaime C. Bulatao, Father Francisco R. Demetrio, Father Leonardo N. Mercado, Dr. Virgilio G. Enriquez, and many others—I hope to honor your memory with my work, which is rooted in yours.

To the reader: I am glad this space has found you. As your soul navigates the streams of the world beyond, I pray you have a safe journey. Return safely home.

-

CHAPTER ONE

Indigenization

An old Filipino proverb says, *Ang hindi marunong lumingon sa pinang-galingan ay hindi makararating sa pinaroroonan.* (Those who do not honor their roots will never reach their destination.) When this *salawikain* (proverb) tells us to "turn" *(lumingon),* I do not think it means that we should walk back to where we came from (that is, *regress*). Rather, we simply ought to acknowledge how far we have come. We will eventually go back home, and by then we will be filled with the wisdom of experience. Our elders might say: *Papunta ka pa lang, pauwi na ako.* (You are still on your way, while I am already on my way home.) And so, the cycle of their hero's journey is complete. We are meeting now at different points in our individual adventures. If you choose to join me, we shall enter the forest of our collective cultural subconscious. There, the bloodthirsty beasts of history roam. We enter anyway, to find the wellspring of ancestral memory. Strengthen your will *(lakas ng loob)* but be open to transformation *(pagbabagong-loob).* As another Filipino proverb goes, *Huwag pumasok sa gubat ang mga taong takot sa ahas.* (Those who are afraid of snakes should not enter forests.)

Shared History

There seems to be a growing awareness today of the need to create more meaningful inclusivity. This means honoring the beauty of world cultures, especially those that have been suppressed, exploited, or destroyed by colonization. These voices have been historically ignored or invalidated. Many of these cultures were considered "less civilized" and were thus seen as being on the lower stage of human psychosocial development. They were believed to be much closer to animal nature than human nature. Some of them were even featured in ethnological expositions or "human zoos," where colonizers showed the "civilized" world how they had "tamed" the "savages."

In 1904, Igorot people from the Philippines were displayed during the St. Louis World's Fair in the United States. This was done to show the world how the natives of the newly acquired US colony needed to be subjugated and educated. By our standards today, this is considered deplorable, and when we are presented with this snapshot of history, we might understandably be angered. But the way this story is often told is one-sided, and ironically, in our well-intentioned desire to speak up about our exploited ancestors, we do not get to hear their actual voices. Listening to the stories of the Bontok people who remember that time, they would say that their journey abroad was in fact also an opportunity for adventure, to see the world beyond their village.[1] The manifestations of racism that they experienced then still seem to occur today—these occasions were of course quite vile but not limited to that time. But, in general, many of them found it to be a good experience, since they were also fed, paid, and toured around. They were also given gifts to bring back home. Whenever they felt cheated or exploited, the Igorots took to the courts and went through the US legal system, which actually ruled in their favor. That is not to say that this suddenly becomes a forgivable historical event. But it should open our eyes to the fact that it is very easy to look at the past and moralize in black and white. After all, the past is dead, so it cannot object to our modern handling of it. We tend to speak up for the dead, rather than listen to hear what they had to say.

The oppression, exploitation, and denigration that our ancestors have gone through are all well-documented. But also, as we tell our own stories, we can challenge the tendency to see ourselves merely as passive objects in history. The danger of this is that we may carry a sense of helplessness with us, and we might then begin to define our identity in terms of how we have suffered rather than how we have persisted and how we have thrived. We know very little about how our precolonial ancestors resisted and successfully defended our lands against the Spanish invaders—Ferdinand Magellan is still believed to be the first person to circumnavigate the globe despite the fact that he and most of his crew were massacred by the native leader Lapu-Lapu. The Ilustrados, who were the upper class during the Spanish colonial era, had written subversive material that inspired mass revolts. Various publications subverted authority, such as Marcelo H. del Pilar's *Dasalan at Tuksuhan* (Prayers and Tricks), which poked fun at the greed and hypocrisy of the corrupt friars. This includes mock-prayers such as *Aba Ginoong Barya* (O Holy Coin), a parody of *Aba Ginoong Maria* (Hail Mary). Jose Rizal's *Noli Me Tangere* is a classic novel that revealed the abhorrent decadence and abuses of the time, and this stoked the existing fire in the hearts of revolutionaries. Historian Reynaldo Ileto has also pointed out how the colonial church intended Jesus Christ's Passion on the cross to teach the natives to accept the suffering on earth for heavenly reward—but the masses took it as a call to be like Christ and fight those who crucify us.[2] At that time, many of our revolutionary leaders were young: They were in their twenties.

The United States offered to "help" us fight against the Spaniards, but in the end, they saw the Philippines as a prize, at least as a way to enter the Asian market. They "won" the Philippines by taking over the war against the Spaniards right when the revolutionary Filipinos were winning— they put a flag up in the walled city of Intramuros, whose defenses had already been weakened by the Filipinos. The United States's "pacification" of the natives took seven long years and left thousands dead—more on the Filipino side, with a ratio of sixteen Filipinos killed per one American.[3] In *Imagining Manila*, Tom Sykes pointed out, echoing Ileto, that the Philippine-American war of 1899 is one that is rarely, if ever, talked about. Sykes exposed literary material during that time that promoted the enterprising spirit of brave American soldiers fighting the "savages" in the jungles of the Philippines, glossing over the atrocities of war that are projected onto the exotic native.[4] These centuries have been, to us, continuous bloody unrest and literary subversion, not mere submission. If we continue to believe that we have always been subservient to the colonial authority out of fear, then we might fall prey to the propaganda that others must liberate us because we cannot save ourselves. Even today, we see ourselves as much weaker than others, not even as the world's younger sibling but as a cat on the side of the road, just watching children play—what we call *saling pusa*. I am not only talking economically, but more so psychologically, and perhaps even spiritually. We must start to recognize our engagement with history as we move through time. We are the descendants of our colonized ancestors, but we are also the grandchildren of revolution. We are travelers and pilgrims, and our identity is never permanently fixed.

In the old days, when a family needed to move residences, the village would come together and help carry their house. We call this *bayanihan,* which today means "camaraderie" and "collaboration," especially in times of distress. Rebuilding homes destroyed by natural disasters is bayanihan. Rescuing refugees fleeing from war zones is bayanihan. During the COVID-19 pandemic, community pantries started popping up on the corners of streets across the country to feed those who were starving during the lockdowns. That is bayanihan. *Bayanihan* also has the words *bayan* (country) and *bayani* (hero), and from this, we can imagine that the willingness to expand our individual identities to encompass the community is the precursor to heroism. Heroism is a kind of strength that persists amid adversity. We tend to think of this power as something that is given to us, usually by outsiders in the form of funds and other resources. We also believe that it can be taken from us. So, for so long, we have limited our strength to the approval and assistance of outsiders.

But in the case of bayanihan, we see that power can emerge from within, and it is shared. We do not have to wait for the permission of others for us to advance; we can carry each other. Accountability on the part of those who wronged us is important, but our own healing should not depend on them. We do not have to follow the outsiders' timeline.

History is *kasaysayan,* from *saysay,* referring to both "story" and "meaning." Something that is considered useless or meaningless is called *walang saysay* (literally, "no meaning" or "no story"). *Kasaysayan* therefore implies collective meaning-making through storytelling. Zeus Salazar said that our history can be written in three ways. The first way is written by an outsider, who talks about our culture only in comparison to theirs. The second way is written by defensive idealists who tend to overly romanticize our culture. They would present our story in a certain way, curating and reframing it to impress outsiders. Both these ways use the outsider as the standard for meaning-making. They are written from the outside looking in. The third way, which Salazar called the Pantayong Pananaw, is the story we tell each other, interpreted through our own ways of knowing.[5] It draws from anecdotes, folklore, and collective memory. It is the insider's understanding. This is a critical approach to the truthfulness of storytellers since many of them want to tell us who we are from their perspective—and this would usually have a hidden motive.

It is very tempting to essentialize everything, to create a dichotomy of us versus them, of friend versus enemy. The reality is much more complicated, but written history is heavily edited. Historians—especially colonial historians—were very selective with which parts to include in history, and they have been very careful to only include those that promote their agenda. Since we trust the fact that documentation is a tangible memory of the past, we think that history books are, by themselves, reliable markers of history. What is written enters mainstream consciousness and becomes part of collective memory—regardless of whether it accurately represents our experiences. And, since many of these books were written by outsiders, our memories are also the outsiders' memories—with themes of their own greatness. The writer Nick Joaquin pointed out that our current conception of the history of the Philippines is just the history of visitors. Rather than focus on how outsiders have changed us, he said, we should look at how we have changed because of what these outsiders brought in—that is, the various tools that have allowed us to better express ourselves.[6] Joaquin pointed out how other cultures have muted the impact of the invaders in their historical narratives, focusing instead on the new technology that entered their culture. Also, these invaders are themselves just "things" we reacted to. It is important, of course, to talk about when and how the colonizers imposed themselves on us—but it is just as important (or even more so) to write the history of how the introduction of the printing press impacted local literature, how ecclesiastical hierarchy influenced the structure of local religious groups, or how foreign political theories influenced our approach to national governance. How, then, did we as a culture become who we are today?

At this point, it is, of course, very difficult to identify which elements of our culture are still "authentic" to us. It is like we are living in an old house that has been renovated multiple times. It may still look like it used to, but most of the materials are new, and the rusty pipes and the planks that have been destroyed by termites have been replaced. It is also like the paradox of the Ship of Theseus, which has been maintained for centuries: Say you had a ship, and as time passes, parts of it begin to rot and break. You would like to preserve this ship, as it carries meaning and memory. So, you have to replace its broken parts one by one until, eventually, all the parts have been replaced. Now, centuries later, is it still the same ship?

On Filipino history, the journalist Carmen Guerrero Nakpil famously said that we have spent three hundred years in a convent and fifty years in Hollywood. I think that, at this point, we have only retained the elements that resonate the most with us. As a melting pot of world culture, Philippine society is like many of our popular dishes, which draw from various foreign influences—fried *lumpia* and *pancit canton* from the Chinese, *kaldereta* from the Spanish, *kare-kare* from the Indians, and so on—yet our cuisine has a distinctly Filipino flavor. Many meals include hotdog slices, while others use corned beef to replace more expensive meat. One of my favorites, pork *sisig*, is a fragrant Kapampangan dish that is perfect with ice-cold native beer. I especially love it when it is crispy and spicy. Sisig is made with the head of pigs, because, historically, that is the portion that was not being used by the cooks of the nearby military air base to feed the US troops. This culinary resilience is also found in our banana ketchup, which was created to supplement the lack of tomatoes during World War II. Banana ketchup is also traditionally used to make Filipino spaghetti. Even the sweet Filipino spaghetti is distinctly Filipino. Nevertheless, all these foreign influences taste like home. The Ship of Theseus implies that identity should exist in its materiality. But the ship is just a symbol; Theseus lives on in the memory of those who continue to reconstruct his legacy. Similarly, whatever materiality culture has is symbolic. Its true meaning is carried by the people.

My Work

I am a Filipino teacher and researcher. I was born and raised in the Philippines, and I currently live here with my family. The Philippines is a multiethnic archipelago with thousands of islands and three major island groups: Luzon, Visayas, and Mindanao. My mother is from Visayas, and my father is from Mindanao (his family, however, came from North Luzon). My parents met in Luzon when they went there to study. I was born in the Visayas, but we moved to Luzon, and we have stayed here ever since. We still frequently visit family in Visayas and Mindanao. I am at the intersection of various island identities, which are all individually Filipino. Our ancestors moved around so much that our cultures often borrowed from each other. Yes, there are still some clear regional distinctions, but I would not go on to say that something is only Ilokano, or only Tagalog, or only Ilonggo. All of it, very broadly speaking, is Filipino. (I will talk more about Filipino-ness and cultural authenticity in chapter 6.)

A huge part of my identity is my spirituality, and this goes beyond affiliations to certain religious institutions. It is a part of everyday life, to the point that, if I did not reflect on my experiences, I would not even notice how mystical they are. I grew up surrounded by deeply religious people. I suppose I am just lucky that many of them were living saints; I know that others are not so lucky, since religion can also be weaponized to maintain restrictive social norms. This is still true, even for me, especially in larger society. But on a personal level, my beliefs are primarily shaped by my mother's folk wisdom. My interactions with other relatives and peers have, of course, also been instrumental in my spiritual formation. Many of them claimed to be able to sense spirits, which were usually lingering ghosts in old houses or elementals in grassy areas. It is fascinating how often Filipinos honor the original inhabitants of a land. People would sometimes whisper that a house was built on a sacred site or cemetery, or that there were already "people" living in this area, and they continue to live as extra inhabitants in a house. *"Sila yung dating nakatira diyan,"* we might say, telling others that the spirits were people who once lived on the land. This implies that spaces have a spiritual history and that we live on an earth that remembers.

Anecdotes of either miraculous or terrifying synchronicities are frequently heard at our dinner tables. Almost every Sunday in my childhood was spent in the house of a relative who was a faith healer. She told me that I may have the potential for healing, but that my power would only reveal itself when I am ready. My family thought I would become a doctor. Other relatives prayed that I would become a priest. Eventually, I entered the mental health field as a psychologist—this, I suppose, is a special kind of healing. This and many other strange experiences are part of who I am, but I have never considered them as evidence I was somehow more special than others. I know more people who have had even more paranormal experiences than not. I consider myself a healthy skeptic, but I know how culturally valuable these experiences are. Investigating these phenomena is one thing, but interpreting them appropriately is another.

We can engage with these symbols as ways to access the deeper, shared, cultural unconscious.

During the 2020 lockdowns, I indulged in the madness of diving into my personal occult interests. I think that the global pause that came with the COVID-19 pandemic allowed people to reflect deeply on what mattered to them. Confronted with the reality of mass death, we began to rediscover our true passions. I learned how to read tarot cards and interpret dreams. Through social media, I met psychics, witches, demonologists, and starseeds (people who believe that they are, on some level, extraterrestrials). At the same time, I was completing my graduate studies. My research was on telepathy. I have always been fascinated with the paranormal. As I went on with my research, I began to see how much of our daily experiences as Filipinos involve, in one way or another, the paranormal. I had always seen this topic from the perspective of Western psychical research. It was only then that I realized how important it is to contextualize this experience. So, my research went in this direction, and in 2022, I started getting into Philippine folklore and ethnic psychology. Later, I started becoming aware of how Filipino cultural values are inherently transpersonal: In the most ideal and properly contextualized way, these values seem to encourage individuals to go beyond themselves and move toward the collective. It was this realization that inspired my return to the spirituality I was raised with.

I started sharing my research on social media, which, to my surprise, gained the attention of thousands of people around the world. When I began, I did not know how important this was. To me it was just about sharing my interests. To many, it was about recovering ancestral memory. Maybe the search for timeless values is one of the existential effects of the COVID-19 health crisis, as we had to face our mortality. I am not saying that any of this is new—of course, the indigenization movement started decades ago. I am just saying that the context has changed, and it seems that the need for it has intensified. As I interacted with more people—fellow scholars and folks from the diaspora—I learned so much more about the wonderful nuances of culture as it manifests across the globe. Many things resonate despite the distance and difference in time zones. I have learned and unlearned many things, and through this, I have managed to identify the scope of my niche. I am very excited to share my reflections with you. Most of what I have written in this book are thoughts that have developed through my deep study and my engagement with others. I have called this way of thinking Sikodiwa, from the words *sikolohiya* (psychology) and *diwa* (essence or spirit). Sikodiwa is a study of consciousness and culture that is guided by concepts and frameworks found in Philippine languages, myths, and symbols. I am greatly inspired by the work done by many great thinkers before me, and as my roots deepen into the ancient earth, my branches reach out into the open sky.

The perspective I offer here comes from the context of my participation in Philippine society. I do not wish to impose my ideas onto anyone; I am just sharing what I have observed, filtered through my personal experience. Also, I do not claim that my understanding can be generalized to *all* ethnolinguistic cultures across the archipelago—nor I do not claim to know the lived experience of Filipinos in the diaspora—but perhaps I can contribute, in my way, to a more relevant and inclusive understanding of our collective human experience. I hope that, as you read this book, you also engage with it from your context. Acknowledge what resonates (and reflect on why) and critically examine what does not. I have assumed that people would not believe in something that did not have some kind of human truth, no matter how ridiculous or wildly misinformed it may seem. Maybe in reading this, you could open yourself to possibility *(bukas-loob)* while also opening your hands *(bukas palad)* to both receive and give. I wrote this on my own, but I did not write by myself: These reflections echo historical, social, and psychological realities, shared by me and the people I love, here and across time. My work also draws inspiration from great scholars who have come before me. The work that I do is a continuation of their legacy. I honor them now as my guides, the *anitos* of my cerebral pantheon. To me, my work is, as poet-philosopher Albert Alejo put it, "reflection as solidarity."

Filipino Psychology

During the Spanish colonial era, one of our national heroes, Jose Rizal, already challenged the colonizers' persistent claim that the natives were "lazy." In his essay "The Indolence of the Filipino," published in 1890, Rizal pointed out that, aside from the obvious sociopolitical limitations the colonizers had imposed on us, our laziness is only apparent because we were being unfairly judged against foreign standards, which do not consider the natural inclinations of the natives. We are hard-working, but maybe not at midday, when the tropical sun is bearing down on us. Unlike cold countries that have to prepare for frigid winter by hoarding resources during fertile seasons, we have access to the fruits of nature year-round—there is no sense of urgency when we are this blessed. Even today, we see that most Filipinos tend to prioritize the pleasure of the present. Work is not separate from leisure, and we might catch fish or harvest rice while singing songs and playing games. Even for many urban workers, a healthy work environment is a vital aspect of modern industry. Understanding these underlying cultural qualities, passed on through generations, can help us make more practical decisions today that can increase our efficiency.[7] This tradition of recontextualizing attitudes and behaviors would become an important theme in the local social sciences as we worked to reclaim our cultural identity.

The indigenization movement in the field of psychology stirred in the 1960s and 1970s, when there was a growing discomfort surrounding the mainstream Anglocentric perspective of the human condition. Returning from his studies abroad, Virgilio Enriquez sought to correct the misalignment between "Western" (that is, Anglocentric) psychology and the native psychology of Filipinos.[8] (I use "Western" here in the ideological sense, not necessarily in the geographical sense.) Thus, the field of

Sikolohiyang Pilipino (Filipino Psychology) was born, and it celebrates its fiftieth year in 2025. It is fascinating that its theories and methods are still incredibly relevant today, and we hope for its increased popularization.

According to Enriquez himself, Sikolohiyang Pilipino is the appropriate interpretation of the Filipino experience, using our own ways of knowing.[9] Historically, outsiders have interpreted our beliefs and behaviors based on the standard of their own culture, creating a hierarchy of what is considered to be more or less "civilized." They have imposed what works for them in a place where Western attitudes and behaviors would not naturally emerge. Culture is the dynamic knowledge gathered and passed on through generations, shaped by human interactions with their environment.[10]

Imagine a culture that has adapted to cold weather. They may learn how to create magnificent fur coats. They might take over a tropical island and hold the natives to cold standards. The natives, who never needed to cover themselves up, except perhaps with light and beautifully designed patterns, would be taught that showing skin is immoral. It becomes a norm that wearing thick fur coats supposedly shows proper manners, even though the tropical heat makes it impractical. This fashion is just bulky, inconvenient, and uncomfortable. That is not to say that fur coats are completely useless; it only means that we ought to use what works. *Decolonization* refers to the removal of foreign concepts and frameworks that have been imposed on us. It is unlearning the need to wear fur coats in summer. *Indigenization* means relearning what once made sense to us. It does not mean totally regressing to the past—rather, it means working with the present. History is used to find context, but we can also consider the ways in which our interactions with outsiders have allowed us to express ourselves better. It is about relearning the old designs and weaving new clothes that fit the weather, utilizing modern tools. While using Western standards in understanding the Filipino experience may lead to misinterpretation, if certain concepts and frameworks are useful to us, it should not matter where they are from.

Of course, I do not mind that my work is categorized within the broader field of Sikolohiyang Pilipino, because I draw so much inspiration from it. But this lens is only one of many approaches, and in a lot of ways my way of thinking diverges from it. The field itself has particular limitations, owing largely to the vagueness of what it means to be Filipino.* I want to reiterate that although I speak from a Filipino experience, this is only one of many features of my humanity. Sikodiwa, as my particular way of thinking, existed within me before I was at all aware of Sikolohiyang Pilipino as an academic approach; early on, I was inspired by work within the field of transpersonal psychology. However, upon discovering multiple overlaps between my way of thinking and Sikolohiyang Pilipino, and upon realizing how transpersonal this field can be, I found it incredibly edifying. In any case, there are multiple entry points to studying our common humanity, including identifying meaningful concepts in our language, observing social dynamics and traditional customs, and surveying folk beliefs. In general, the concepts and frameworks we use, especially in the study of Philippine culture, come from commonsense psychology *(kinagisnang sikolohiya),* or the ingrained knowledge of the ordinary Filipino embedded in aesthetics, beliefs, and customs.[11]

Language

My use of English to write this book is a practical choice: I know that I am writing for a larger audience. Therefore, I will speak in the language I know that is most understood by whoever I am talking to. I find that the English language can be used with clinical precision to take things apart and inspect them—we understand that each word is distinct from other words. Unfortunately, there is not much room for context; most of

---

* For example, any discussion of a "Filipino personality," or Pagkataong Pilipino, necessarily requires some kind of generalizing essentialism that ignores intersectional identities.

the time, what is written and said must be clear and direct. However, it is important to understand that I will not be simply translating Filipino terms into English. As much as possible, I will use the local term. The reason is that many of these concepts are high in context, and although they have a general meaning, they may change depending on how they are used.

Anyone studying Filipino grammar will attest to its incredible complexity. Frankly, I do not think that what language I use matters at all, as long as I am able to communicate what I mean. A person can be fluent in any of the Philippine languages, but if they are coming from a foreign worldview, then they are simply importing their ideologies, much like the colonizers did when they introduced their religious dogma and sociocultural values. If, on the other hand, the speaker comes from a folk worldview, the language that they use will only be one of many ways through which they can express their truth.

The concepts I will be using here are concepts that I know personally and frequently use. I will not be appropriating concepts from ethnolinguistic groups that I am not part of. That said, it is true that most of the concepts used in current academic and literary discourse come from the Tagalog language. There are more than a hundred distinct languages in the Philippines. Although the nationalized "Filipino" language supposedly includes all languages and dialects across the archipelago, it is, in its current form, often interchangeable with Tagalog. We might feel like this is an imposition of one ethnolinguistic group to everyone else. It feels that Manila, being the capital of the Philippines, is at the center of culture. This has been an issue ever since Filipino was enshrined as the national language in the 1987 Constitution. (English is, by the way, also considered to be the other constitutionally approved "official" language used in education, communication, and law.) Article XIV, Section 6 of the 1987 Constitution encourages the continued evolution of the Filipino language based on existing languages in use in the Philippines. The criticism we might have today of Tagalog being the default form of Filipino is not new; heated discourse around it existed when it was first announced. Many pointed out that this may overshadow other local languages, others said that Filipino has not evolved enough to be an official language for legal or educational purposes, and others asked whether this is appropriate, considering that Tagalog had not yet been accepted by everyone. Around this time, there was intense political unrest in the country. News of coups and disasters was broadcast in Tagalog to the entire nation, with individual local stations reporting in their areas in their native language.

As Filipino professor Efren Abueg pointed out, the language we use in our discourses should be the language that people can understand, and, even in non-Tagalog regions, Tagalog is understood. It is practical, therefore, to just call it Filipino, since it reaches across the archipelago.[12] Whenever a person travels to the far south, they can still use Filipino in most places and ask for directions when lost. When they travel to Batanes, in the northernmost part of the Philippines, they can turn the television on and watch the national news in Filipino. When they go to a different country, and their soul recognizes a fellow Filipino, their initial interaction will most likely be in Filipino. Perhaps it is only while they are talking that they would notice an accent from a certain region. My parents are great at picking up when someone they are talking to is Bisaya. They would then confirm it with the person, and they would continue the conversation in their native tongue. Interestingly, a lot of Bisaya terms are found in general usage, even in mental health discourse, such as the words *ginhawa* (breath, which we have standardized in academic discourse as "well-being") and *buang* ("madman"). The practical fact is that the national language constantly absorbs a multitude of words that are useful in expressing national sentiments, and it is broadcast throughout the country in various media. That is not to say that we should dissolve every other language, but rather encourage the inclusion of them all.

Now, so far, I have only talked about the sociopolitical concerns surrounding the national language. But this book is not about creating the ideal nation. I have no intention of insisting on a "perfect" or "pure"

Filipino. Instead, in this book, I will be using language as a psychological access point. Since we use language to express our everyday experiences, we can look at the language we use as a map to the cultural inner world— and in order to do this, I cannot impose the "right" language; I must be open to hearing what is being used by people on the street day-to-day. So, as I write this book, I will be using the language that I am most familiar with. Being that this is an expression of my current thinking, I would rather not pretend to be fluent in any other language just to meet some superficial political-aesthetic standard. If I were to talk about the authenticity of personal and cultural expression, I would want to be authentic myself. In any case, Filipino is also the language that most Filipinos can understand. That is what language is for, after all. I earnestly hope that this work will eventually be made available in other languages as well, but I should hope that one who is more fluent in that language could do the more appropriate, nuanced translation. As I speak in both English and Filipino, I apply the psychosocial nuances I am familiar with, which these languages have allowed me to access.

Some purists may not agree with me regarding this approach. I once used the word *mundo* to refer to the universe. Someone correctly pointed out that this was a Spanish term, and that the better term would be *sansinukob* (universe). There are other terms too, such as *sanlibutan, santinakpan,* or *daigdig.* All of these are deep, beautiful, and somewhat archaic terms, popularly used in lengthy religious rites and cerebral Filipino novels. I suppose it is just a matter of preference. I used *mundo* in the way that we use it today. A corny poet might say, *"Ikaw ang aking daigdig!"* (You are my world!) We would applaud them for being *makata* (poetic), but it would feel too dusty and Shakespearean. But I would sing to my lover, *"Ikaw ang mundo ko."* These statements mean the same thing, but I would feel more grounded with the second one. We have already borrowed so many foreign words to express ourselves better. From Spanish, we have words like *kumusta* (from *como esta,* a greeting), *biyahe* (from *viaje,* meaning "journey"), and even *harana* (from *jarana,* a serenade).

From Sanskrit, we have words like *guro* (from *guru*, meaning "teacher"), *agham* (from *agama*, meaning "knowledge"), and *diwa* (from *jiva*, meaning "life force" or "soul"). From Hokkien, we have *ate* (older sister), *ginto* (gold), *suki* (returning buyer), and a host of food-related terms like *lumpia, pansit, goto,* and *lomi.* We also create our own definitions of English words, such as "comfort room" or CR, which refers to a toilet, and "commute" or *komyut,* which in our usage refers to any form of travel that specifically uses public transportation. We Filipinize foreign terms that have no direct translation, such as *kompyuter* and *apir* (from "up here," as in "high five"). Most of us are also comfortable mixing English and Filipino in our casual conversations, which just shows our creative linguistic adaptations to whatever social context we are placed in. All that being said, it seems that our language carries the implicit codes to our shared psychology and memory. Concepts drawn from our language are doorways to greater mysteries, and in this book, we are more interested about what is behind these doors, rather than what the doors look like.

Universality

To be clear, this book is not a textbook on Filipino psychology or Sikolohiyang Pilipino. I like to think of my work as a study of *human* psychology, guided by Filipino cultural concepts. In other words, even if a concept seems to appear uniquely in Filipino psychology, that does not mean that *only* Filipinos can experience it. It is a human potential that can be applied anywhere, by anyone. But that also does not mean that I am creating a universal theory. I am not presenting folk psychology as an alternative to mainstream psychology—that would be too ambitious! I only hope to expand our perceived limitations of what the human experience is supposed to be. Historically, our psychology has been interpreted through an outsider's perspective, and so many concepts have been distorted, usually to suit a colonial agenda. But there is a wealth of psychospiritual wonder here, and I hope we can bring that to light.

Furthermore, I would also like to make it clear that I have no intention of antagonizing our foreign allies, nor do I want to promote some kind of idealized national identity. This closes us off from the global community. I only think that it is important to contextualize our experiences in our particular memory and worldview and contribute our take on what it means to be human, operating within historical, sociocultural, and political systems that have emerged from our interactions with the world. If anything, the potentially uncomfortable historical anecdotes that will be discussed in this book can show us our growing pains, the bruises, and scars that make us who we are today. We do this in the same way we might revisit our own diaries and photo albums to get a grasp of why we are the way we are. It is a conversation with ourselves, past, present, and forevermore.

For the Filipino, wherever you are around the globe, I hope that this book can, at the very least, be an affirmation of who you are. But this book is not just for us; I am not gatekeeping these concepts from non-Filipinos. *Gatekeeping* implies that something is a property (that is, we hide it behind a gate). I do not own these experiences, concepts, and frameworks—these memories and reflections are not specific to me. I am only connecting the dots and showing you patterns that I hope could be useful to personal and collective liberation. What you are reading, then, is my way of knowing, the flow of my thoughts. Of course, not all of these will resonate with everyone, and that is fine; I will not insist on anything. These are only offerings that have been very useful to me. I would love to imagine all of us—Filipinos and non-Filipinos—learning from each other and applying best practices toward a more inclusive world. We must value the collaborative cocreation of knowledge over the mere extraction of data. Let me now offer you what I know, so that you can fill in what you know—in this way, we can participate in a dialogue of people showing up as themselves.

CHAPTER TWO

-

Cultural Identity

I am not the arbiter of Filipino culture. Unfortunately, anyone who picked up this book up hoping for a clear checklist to identify what a Filipino is will probably be disappointed—though I hope, after sitting with these uncomfortable nuances, they will be enlightened. For everyone else, I hope, most of all, that what you find here is the comfort of home.

In the discussions I have had over the years with different folks from the diaspora, the main question surrounding culture seems to be: Am I Filipino enough? This is an interesting question because it implies there is a person who is the "*most* Filipino." I struggle to imagine what that person might look like, but if we want to play this game, we will have to assume some kind of "pure" atom of Filipino-ness. This person, whoever they may be, would be solely Filipino: they would have to be native to the land, and decolonized (or never colonized at all). Their beliefs, customs, language, and cuisine should all come from the Filipino community. Ironically, what I am describing is not Filipino at all: It is a caricatured absurdity outside of human time, devoid of all historical and sociopolitical context. Besides, no culture emerges from a vacuum, as nothing much would survive in sealed isolation. We all come from the land, and we all move across the earth—our great continents are, themselves, lands that moved. The more comfortable we are with diversity and the more open we are to *both* the struggle and resilience of our ancestors, the better we can understand that culture is just a manifestation of humanness, and Filipino-ness is just one of many wonderful ways to be human.

Cultural Lens

I have always been fascinated by the spiritual reaches of human psychology—and I do love the way someone once described my work as "psycho-mystical." I suppose this means that my work is grounded in everyday experience (psycho-) while also transcending the isolating tendency of individuality (-mystical). I am a researcher, which, by definition, means that I do not know everything: I look (that is, "search"), and then I look again to determine if I found the right thing ("re-search"). My research interests are informed by my upbringing, having been surrounded by creative and deeply spiritual people. This is the reality I am used to, and I do see how miracles can happen to those who align their worldview to that which affirms its possibility. There is nothing specifically religious about any of these beliefs. They go beyond the solid stone hierarchies of Catholic mythology, and they weave through the jungle of folk beliefs. They just are.

As I said, I grew up practicing a variety of religious customs, and I would say that it can be fundamentally difficult to distinguish which is superstition and which is genuinely spiritual. I define *superstition* as "that which is compulsively done yet is not grounded in real-world practicalities." I define *spirituality* as "existentially meaningful echoes of our relationship with the world." However, since we change with the world, it could be that the set of beliefs that we now call "superstition" are just atrophied versions of what was once a highly potent spirituality. In other words, it probably worked for our ancestors, allowing them to access psycho-mystical realms of consciousness that genuinely assisted them in their everyday lives. With environmental and social changes, maybe these practices no longer work the way they used to. (Except, in certain sacred sites, such as Mount Banahaw, where visitors who do not follow the guidance of the locals are said to get lost, both physically and mentally, even today.) Culture is the undercurrent of curiosity and adaptability that allows humans to gather knowledge about their physical and social environments. This knowledge, which shapes our shared identity, is key to our survival and sanity. It is passed on through the generations. As cultures interact with other cultures, they freely borrow knowledge from each other as a way to continue their own evolution. Environments may change, and so certain cultural beliefs and practices may no longer be effective.

All this considered, I just *happened* to be born Filipino. As far as I know, I did not consciously choose to be born Filipino, yet I am, and so, the lens through which I understand the universal realities accessible to all people is shaped in this particular sociocultural context. The manifestations of psycho-mystical phenomena that I experience are distinctly Filipino not because they only happen to Filipinos, but because our cultural systems of knowledge allow us to easily recognize, understand, and invoke these experiences in the way that we know them. In other words, nothing about what I do is "purely" Filipino at all, in that only Filipinos can experience these social attitudes and folkloric encounters. For example, let us look at the belief in *engkanto,* an entity that appears across the archipelago in various forms, an entity that lures humans into the forest. Someone who is *"na-engkanto"* (influenced by an engkanto) might experience memory loss and altered behavior, much like one who is experiencing, what we call in psychiatry, dissociation. Now, this ingkanto syndrome (as folklorist Herminia Meñez called it)[1] is not unique to Filipinos—the local engkanto has parallels to the fae of European folklore, and even to the extraterrestrials and the abductions of people found in modern American folklore. It is interesting to note also that in pretechnological encounters, the supernatural kidnappers live on the earth (or at least in a parallel earthlike realm), whereas in modern folklore, since we have been exposed to the unimaginable horrors of space, they now live outside it.

Beyond folklore, when we look at social attitudes like *kapwa* (shared identity) and *loob* (interiority), we tend to think that they are uniquely

Filipino. Placed in context to identify their nuances and social implications, it can be said that these concepts emerged naturally from culture. But they can also occur to different people, Filipino or non-Filipino, beyond the archipelago, across geographical boundaries, and may manifest in a variety of wonderful contexts. We might have different names for them: kapwa psychology does have many similarities with the African concept of *ubuntu,* which may be defined as the affirmation of one's humanity through the recognition of others'.[2] The philosophy of loob, as described by great Filipino scholars such as writer Reynaldo Ileto, poet Albert Alejo, and philosopher Leonardo Mercado, seems to echo Taoist philosophy, in that the individual finds harmony in following the innate wisdom within oneself that aligns with all of nature. One might even go as far as to point out how the wholeness of one's loob *(buo ang loob)* aligns with divine will *(loob ng Maykapal)* in very much the same way as the Hindu concept of atman (individual self) and brahman (absolute reality). Proponents of perennial philosophy, most especially the writer Aldous Huxley, have pointed out that many world religions rest on the fundamental idea that you are the divine ground manifested in its fragmented form.[3] In an essay on loob, Alejo pointed out that looking into one's loob doesn't reveal more of oneself, but more of other people. We are, so he says, like scattered islands, but deep in the waters, we see that we are all connected.[4] Within loob is kapwa.

So, the distinctions made across regions and ethnolinguistic groups, between mainlanders and diaspora, are just various cultural expressions and interpretations of the same human realities. To learn more, we must travel, read, immerse, and converse. To me, there is no need to fully integrate anything into one singular identity, at least on a psychological level, because doing so erases any sense of real identity. When we truly think about it, that is the agenda of colonialism, wherein differences are absorbed into one larger thing, dissolving and even suppressing any variety. However, the opposite tendency, to segregate and impose boundaries and hierarchies, is both impractical and dangerous, for no one lives alone, and isolation only leads to death. Besides, any form of segregation is artificial because, in reality, we know that identities overlap. In segregation, too many exceptions must be made with the caveat that "I am this, but I am also that, etcetera. . . . " We will soon have to realize that differences strengthen personal identity, yet, at the same time, it is only through others that we truly know ourselves.

Cosmic Origins

Our seafaring ancestors traveled from one island to another, trading resources and sharing their stories and traditions. The stories we have about our cosmic origins hold clues as to how we understand the purpose and meaning of the human experience. There are multiple creation myths across the archipelago, but it seems that many of them share similar themes. Perhaps, if we are looking for cultural identity, mythology could be a great place to begin.

There are various names for the creator deity, but today they are popularly known as Bathala. The name Bathala is said to come from the Sanskrit word for "noble lord."[5] In Negros, the name is Laon, which means "ancient one." Other texts may use the name Abba, but this is a mistranslation on the part of the early chroniclers, because they assumed that it referred to "father" when it is just an exclamatory word.[6] Even today, we still use "Aba!" to denote surprise, disbelief, or wonder. The Hail Mary prayer is translated as *Aba Ginoong Maria,* or "Hail Noble Mary." A child who answers back at their parents might hear the phrase, *"Aba, sumasagot ka na!"* (Ah, so you have learned how to answer back!) A friend who witnesses another friend's personal transformation might say, with awe, *"Aba, ibang tao ka na!"* (Well, well, well, you have become a different person!) A shopper who did not expect a special item to be on sale might say, *"Aba, mura lang oh!"* (Wow, look at how cheap this is!) It is also interesting to note that, about the gender of the almighty, they are not all male with long flowing beards—Laon is often considered female. In some religious sects, Bathala may be called Amang Bathala, or Father God. This may very well imply the deification of masculinity, as it is with most patriarchal religions, but it may also be the *humanization* of the divine, in that Bathala is approachable precisely because he is our father.[7] (This, I think, is closer to the true biblical purpose of seeing the Abrahamic God as a father, compared to the political masculinity of godhood.) Perhaps this is also the same reason why there is a strong Marian devotion in the Philippines, not mainly because of gendered power, but because of matriarchal family values.

Another name for the creator deity is Maykapal, which directly translates to "the authority." When a person acts in an arrogant or entitled manner, we say, *"Ang kapal ng mukha!"* (Their face is so thick!) This implies the question, What gives them the right to act in this way? But also, when a friend of ours is too timid to ask for what they deserve, we advise them to thicken their face: *"Kapalan mo lang mukha mo."* *Kapal* is a word that refers to thickness, and so if someone inherently has it, they have the right to do or say anything. There are other more specific names, such as Kabuniyan (the great teacher of the Cordillera region) and Melu (the Blaan creator deity from whose dead skin we were molded). In Bukidnon, there is Diwata na Magbabaya (roughly translated as "the divinity who wills all things"). *Diwata* is a term that is found among various ethnolinguistic groups; it has Hindu-Buddhist origins and refers generally to any divine being or spirit. Today, we use this word to refer to a fairy or a beautiful woman. In the Philippines, generally speaking, then, it seems that most of our names for the creator deity are just descriptors for that vague, meta-cosmic, supernatural power—we know that whoever they are, they are ancient and noble, and they inspire wonder.

A Pan-Philippine Creation Myth

What follows is my preferred narrative of the creation myth, woven from various stories. This story is inspired by the tales collected by Francisco

Demetrio, Damiana Eugenio, and F. Landa Jocano from the documented accounts of European chroniclers and colonial anthropologists, as well as surviving oral traditions.[8] I have, of course, taken creative liberties here, as this is the story that personally resonates the most with me.

Many myths tell us that the sky and sea have existed since the beginning. However, the sky was so low that the sun was burning Maykapal's face. So, they poked one of the sun's eyes and pushed the sky up to its current height. Maykapal had a pet bird, Manaul, that had beautiful colored feathers. In some stories, Manaul was a king who was entrenched in conflict with another king. Manaul was allowed to fly across the vast cosmos. This cosmic bird appears in various folktales. The early Tagalogs listened to a particular blue bird, which they called Tigmamanukin, for omens. Among the Maranao, the Sarimanok, a colorful cosmic bird, is a common motif in folk art. The Mangyan believe that humans came from the egg of the Limokon. The Bagobo also understand the Limokon as a bird whose song is an omen. Among folk Catholics, Saint Peter is said to hold a rooster (Manok ni San Pedro). In the folk Christian creation myth, which was written down by the Melencio T. Sabino in the 1955 occult book *Karunungan ng Dios* (Wisdom of God), the creator deity, Infinito Dios, is depicted as a cloaked eye with wings. The folkloric interest in this bird seems to tie into the practice of cockfighting *(sabong)*, which was a popular pastime among our ancestors (it still is today, especially among gamblers). The Sulodnon believe that, upon death, they would visit a cockpit *(sabungan)* where they can place a bet.

It is interesting to note that we have many idioms surrounding *manok* (chicken). If something is easy, we say that it is like a chick *(sisiw)*. My father would say that something is "chicken feed" if it can be done quickly and with little effort. Someone's protege—or whoever they are rooting for in any competition—is their manok (that is, their bet in a cockfight). When life is difficult, and we are working only to sustain ourselves, we say that our life is *"Isang kahig, isang tuka"* (one scratch, one peck). The philosopher Leonardo Mercado used the cockfight as a metaphor for

Filipino culture.[9] In the sabungan, he said, everyone is equal, and everyone has a bet in the ring. We also bet on our friend's manok, therefore extending our personal identity to include them. Relationships are contagious and interconnected; when one is affected by either loss or success, everyone else is as well. The practice of sabong may be bloody and cruel, but, philosophically, it shows our attitudes toward fate. We can care for our manok, feed and train it right, but, when it comes to the battles of life, we will eventually have to trust in things that we cannot control. We will have to listen to omens.

Returning now to the creation myth, we see Manaul eventually getting tired and in need of a place to rest, but there was nowhere to lie down. So, it splashed some seawater onto the sky. The sky worried that the sea was rising too high, so it pinned the sea down with islands. Finally, Manaul was able to rest, and in its sleep, it dreamed of the entire history of the world.

One day, the gorgeous sea breeze, Maguayen, was walking on the surface of the water. The fragrant land breeze, Kaptan, saw her and greeted her. "Hello, beautiful bubble of the sea." Maguayen gave him a mocking smile and turned away. This mythic encounter, drawn from the mythology of the Visayans and recorded by José Maria Pavón, was always amusing to me. In this story, Kaptan comes across as charming but arrogant, and this is an attitude we call *mahangin* (windy) or, in more casual terms, *presko*. If the day is sunny but the breeze flows strong and cool, we also say that it is presko.

So, Kaptan, undeterred, firmly stood before Maguayen and said, "I do not mean to annoy you, but it is only you and I here, and I would love to make your acquaintance."

Maguayen said, "Who are you to speak to me? Do you not know that I can raise the tides of the ocean higher than the tallest mountains?"

Suddenly, there was a flash of lightning. Kaptan said, "Did you see that? That is one of my loyal servants."

Startled, Maguayen exclaimed, "Leave me or else be taken by the sea!"

A wave crashed on Kaptan. He fell but immediately regained his balance and apologized profusely for shocking her with the lightning. He admitted that he only wanted to display his power. Despite her reaction, Maguayen was impressed by his agility.

"I have long wondered whether there was a being with power equal to mine," Maguayen said. "I have many proteges in the depths of the sea, and my will commands the waves."

Kaptan replied, "It is by my breath that the clouds are filled with rain, and this nourishes all life. By my signal, lightning strikes, and when I move, so does the wind. I offer all these powers to you, along with my undying affection."

And so they were married, and as a mark of their love a bamboo was planted on the land. Manaul saw this and was curious about it, so it pecked the bamboo. From it emerged the first people. They were fruitful and multiplied. Maykapal taught them all they needed to know, and the humans passed this knowledge on to their children, and so on, through the generations.

Where We Come From

We experience time linearly, so when we talk about "origins," we tend to trace it back to the beginning of everything, as if history is a thread that can be pulled until it stops. This is probably why one popular science fiction motif is parallel universes—a model that is quite messy in terms of the little differences that often go unnoticed. This modern myth tells us that our life branches out into a variety of infinite possibilities, in that every moment has endless alternatives. However, our consciousness—that is, our subjective awareness of the world—moves through the labyrinth of potential and experiences only one flow of time, like Ariadne's thread that allowed the ancient Greek hero Theseus to navigate the monster's maze. In the old story, the hero Theseus entered the labyrinth to slay the minotaur, the beast controlled by the king. His daughter, Ariadne, fell in love with Theseus, and helped him navigate the maze with a thread. Our lived experience of time is like this labyrinth, and our consciousness follows this thread. But the thread is not the point; the point is our ability to navigate the cosmic mysteries.

In Philippine folklore, it is often just assumed that certain things already existed, such as the sky and the sea, beyond the limited human perception of linear time. Most of us know the story of the humans from the bamboo, but, as I mentioned earlier, the Mangyan believed that we came from the Limokon's egg—and now we can ask, which came first, the Limokon or their egg? We are trapped in this endless search backward that, like Saint Thomas Aquinas, we are forced, for the sake of argument, to assume a very first thing (or, more formally, a prime mover) that started it all. I once spoke to an occultist who asked me, "If there is a 'God the Father' and a 'God the Son,' then there must be a 'God the Mother,' and a 'God the Grandfather.'" Who—or what—created the Creator? Our folklore seems to ignore these logical absurdities and just assumes that there were already things before we came to be. A child just comes from their parents, and, at least to the child, their parents have been alive *forever.* So, rather than looking at time as one line, we can imagine it as a cosmic tree—we are the leaves that grow from it, but even as we emerge currently, the ancient roots still exist simultaneously with us. We are all that came before and we will be part of everything that will come after us, and all of it is one living organism.

In Filipino, the "indigenous" is called *katutubo,* from the word *tubo* (to grow). One's homeland is their *tinubuang lupa,* or the ground they grew from. In business, *tubo* also refers to profit. *Tubo* can also refer to something long and cylindrical, as in *tubo ng kawayan* (bamboo pole). *Ka* is a prefix that often implies a shared identity, much like the English *co-*. We, the indigenous, grew from the land, like the bamboo, which emerged from the love of the sea breeze and land breeze. We share this indigeneity. It is important, however, to distinguish this from *Indigenous* with a capital *I,* which refers to protected cultures and communities that have somehow resisted colonial influence. So, whenever I refer to the indigenous, I simply refer to what grows naturally from the land we cultivate.

The old nursery rhyme goes: *Bahay kubo, kahit munti, ang halaman doon ay sari-sari...* (Although the nipa hut is small, the plants that grow around it are varied.) Whatever we nourish is what blooms, and that is also what nourishes us. *Katutubo*, then, implies a shared identity of being from the land. But just because one was not born here does not mean that they no longer share our ancestral lineage—a mango grown elsewhere can look different, but it will still taste sweet. We can carry our heritage in our blood, wherever we are *(nasa dugo)*.

Shared Humanity

We have seen, through mythology, that our humanity comes from a shared source. We are human, regardless of space or time; we are only different in the way we express our humanness. We all emerged from the primordial bamboo, as a manifestation of the love of gods. Our language says a lot about what is implied about being human. In particular, we know that something "inhuman" (that is, not human) is either fundamentally different from us (for example, extraterrestrials, monsters, ghouls, and so on) or someone who is cruel, often to an extreme or unnecessary degree. Then to be "human" is to be compassionate and empathic, even if it is only because we share the same basic anatomy. In the spirit of Shakespeare, we might say: Prick me, and I too will bleed.

In Filipino, the word we use to refer to a human being is *tao*. This word is generally understood across the archipelago, as equivalents are present in multiple Philippine languages. In folk belief, the carved idol that represents spirits and deities *(anito)* is called *taotao* or *tatao*. All these words—*tao, tatao,* and *anito*—seem to share the same Malayo-Polynesian root, *tu,* which likely refers to honor or respect.[10] *Tao* is present in the words *katauhan* (humanness) and *katawan* (body), implying that, perhaps, one's humanity is experienced through the body.[11] Furthermore, in our indigenous psychology, one's personality is not simply a social mask (that is, a persona, such as those worn by the ancient theater actors). The individual expression of being is called *pagkatao*, which is the essence of being human.[12] This asserts a shared psychology of belongingness as opposed to an individualistic facade.

Everyday usage of the word *tao* can reveal its inherent qualities. When a person gets hurt, and this offense goes unnoticed, they might say, *"Tao rin ako"* (I am, like you, also human), calling for compassion. Maybe someone's joke went a little too far and it hit a little too close to someone's insecurities. Maybe too many people have offloaded their anger and misery onto one person, and that person has been absorbing too much secondhand trauma and carrying too much emotion. *Tao rin ako.* I also get hurt. Please give me the same care that you might also need for yourself. Help me carry this burden. This, if you remember, is the principle of bayanihan, and on a personal level, we see this in the act of *saluhan* (catching each other), or *sagutan* (answering each other). Maybe you do not have enough money for the lunch you ordered, even though you thought you did. *Sagot na kita* (I will answer for you), so that we can still eat together. Maybe something went wrong with the project you are handling, and regardless of whose fault it is, you are going to suffer an overly harsh consequence. *Sasaluhin kita* (I will catch you), so that you do not suffer alone. This sense of shared responsibility, called *pananagutan*, comes from the understanding that a burden is heavier when carried alone; and because you are human like me, I will carry it with you.

A subtle variation of this phrase is heard when a person makes a mistake: they might excuse themselves by saying, *"Tao lang ako"* (I am only human). Maybe too many accusations or responsibilities are being hurled at one person—stop, please, *tao lang ako!* Maybe, due to hunger, sleeplessness, or stress, a person said or did something that damaged their relationships or reputation. Waking up to their new miserable reality, they desperately seek forgiveness—please understand, *tao lang ako. . . .* The ability to forgive others, *pagtawad*, is to erase any wrongdoing. *"Wala iyon. Huwag mo na isipin."* (It was nothing. Do not think of it anymore.) Interestingly, we also use the word *tawad* when we ask for a discount at a store—but this is more appropriate if the customer already has a relationship with the merchant, such that the merchant would be comfortable "forgiving" any payment "owed" by the customer.

It is difficult to forgive, and it is difficult to recognize the humanity of others. Yet it is in doing so that we participate in shared humanity. As the popular saying goes: *"Madaling maging tao, mahirap magpakatao"* (It is easy to be a human being, but difficult to act like one). *Tao,* then, refers to one's fundamental and embodied being, which deserves respect and understanding.

Searching for Filipino-ness

Despite the recognition of our shared humanity, we still seek a sense of belongingness that can only be found in exclusivity. It is too abstract to belong to *all humans,* and we do know intuitively that there are differences in how we express and understand our humanness. A popular continuation of the creation myth is that the children of the first human parents became lazy and would uselessly lounge about in the house. Having already tried everything they could to inspire their children to make something of themselves, the parents were running out of options. Finally, they decided to threaten them with violence. This effectively moved the children. Many fled and traveled beyond the sea, while others hid inside the house. Some hid in secret rooms, others went into the walls, while others hid near the fireplace. It is believed that those who went into the rooms became the island chiefs, whereas those who went into the walls became ordinary men and slaves. Those who went into the fireplace received a darker complexion, whereas those who fled came back as pale foreigners. In this story, we are all siblings. While we define ourselves as different races, our separation is just the product of distance and time. This ancient story is not too far from how we understand evolution today, which involves the varied mutation of the same species across different geographical locations.*

Again, I am speaking on a psychological and communal level—it is very different on a sociopolitical or legal level because there is a need to be absolutely clear, through binary and causal logic (even though we know intuitively that reality is not limited to these). In other words, one can be Filipino by nationality yet act in ways that may be considered foreign or Westernized. Or one can be understood as more Filipino than certain locals yet be of a different nationality. This begs the question: Is there a hierarchy of Filipino-ness? Are some people more Filipino than others? Are some people less? In popular consciousness, we want to believe that the answer is "Yes." Whoever among us wants to be the judge of what is and is not Filipino necessarily engages in stereotypes, and on this note, we might point out two criteria: *history* and *context*.

HISTORICAL CRITERIA

First, regarding the historical criteria, we might ask the question: "Not considering colonial influence, is this trait or technology something our ancestors would have had?" This implies that true decolonization is somehow a regression into a primitive state, yet it does not provide any distinction as to which era of the precolonial we ought to emulate. It is therefore a form of romanticizing the exotic. I will discuss this more in chapter 6 when I talk about cultural authenticity. It also implies that, somehow, culture is static and fossilized in stone when we know that culture is the dynamic interaction of people with their environment. Our culture is that which is transformed by our interaction with new

---

* To be clear, this should not be misconstrued to imply social Darwinism, wherein oppressed classes and cultures are believed to be on the lower end of the survival of the fittest. Historically, we have seen how violence and domination can be fully intentional, and we have also seen how one of the greatest tools of human survival has been empathy and collaboration against predators and the unpredictable elements. I am only talking about the magnificent persistence of life and its adaptation to various environments.

technology—especially by how we assimilate or resist foreign imports (for example, language, religion, cuisine) in the expression of our collective authenticity.

Leonardo Mercado used the metaphor of a boat.[13] In a fishing community, they used to sing as they went out to catch fish. These beloved songs were passed on through generations. Eventually, the boats became motorized, and the noise of the motor drowned out the music. They continue to fish, this time using larger boats, but the old songs have been forgotten. We can lament this loss while also recognizing the continued use of boats and the human need to fish. Culture is not only defined by what it has lost but also by how it persists. Yes, many of our historical artifacts and ancestral practices have indeed been lost in time due to the recklessness of outside forces or the willful actions of dangerous powers. The reclamation of hope is a radical act. We must realize that we are more than what we have lost. The manifestations of culture are like the honey of bees: It is the expression of who we are, and we will continue expressing ourselves because that is our nature. In this sense, I do agree with Virgilio Enriquez when he said that Filipino culture is "invulnerable."[14]

It is not lost on me that the word *Filipino* is itself an import, the descriptor used by Spanish colonists living in Felipinas, which was named after their king. Natives were simply called *indio*. Eventually, the consciousness of the native elite awakened to the fact that they were the ones born on these islands, and so they deserved the name "Filipino" more than the colonists did. They then used it to refer to themselves, much to the annoyance of the colonial authority.[15] So, "Filipino" eventually became our name, solidified in our constitution out of historical significance and political convenience. During the time of Ferdinand Marcos Sr., there was a serious call to rename our country to Maharlika, which is believed to be the noble class of precolonial natives. It is not; *maharlika* just means "free men," in that they are not slaves *(alipin)*.[16] The Maharlika mythology persists today, especially when online myth-making surrounding the 2022 presidential election has revived the old revisionist mythologies of the Philippines as belonging to the once powerful Maharlika Kingdom, the existence of which no archaeologist has fully confirmed.[17]

We might then look at Indigenous people to study traditions that are relatively unaffected by colonial influence. But to say that they are "more Filipino" ironically forces that foreign term onto them. At the same time, not including them in our shared identity would create a gap in the historical understanding of our heritage. These cultures must be protected, and we have to resist the urge to exoticize them in the same way that the old orientalists did, by portraying them unfairly and appropriating their cultural aesthetics. The study of Filipino psychology must broaden our view of "Filipino" culture, beyond the imperial bastion of old Manila. Yet even Manila is part of what makes us Filipino. "Indigenous," then, can start to apply to all aspects of the culture that emerges naturally from a particular environment, from the local term *katutubo,* which means that which grows (tubo) from the land.

Therefore, Filipino culture is not just how it transformed through history; it is also how it is imbibed by those whose lived reality manifests this transformation. We move on to the next criteria: the contextual.

CONTEXTUAL CRITERIA

When considering the contextual criteria, we might ask: "Does this attitude, aesthetic, philosophy, and so on emerge from the Philippine social context?" There is a heavy implication here that only culture in the Philippines is "truly Filipino." Politically speaking, the line is clear: The Philippines has geographical boundaries, and legal citizenship defines who is Filipino. But culturally, genetically, and socioeconomically, we know that there are many, many variations of what *Filipino* can imply. One can be born with parents who are Filipino citizens yet not themselves be Filipino, either by citizenship or by societal context. We cannot deny that there are differences in culture. This shows the wonder of human ingenuity in how we have survived in a variety of locations across the planet. It shows the resilience of our elders or the limitations of their time. These survival mechanisms are passed on through generations, shaping our beliefs, customs, and institutions.

Mid-century scholarship was generally aware of the supposed differences between East and West. Today, we talk about the cultures of the Global South. These are meaningful distinctions that unfortunately slide into essentialisms—it is through stereotypes that we humans first learn about cultural differences, but it is through proper immersion and discourse that we realize how much more alike we truly are. Nevertheless, we can say that, intuitively, Filipino culture is somehow different from what we broadly consider to be Western culture. Our sociocultural, political, and economic contexts shape what we prioritize, which means that our trends, values, and even sense of humor depend on where we are coming from.

In our local media and scholarship, "West" refers to North America and a vague sense of Europe—that is, the colonial powers whose influence in our lands solidified the distinction between "native" and "foreign." Thus, despite the localization of Western imports, we can still distinguish between what is and is not ours. Many Filipinos today, who have easy access to Western media, private education, and globalized experiences, tend to be more Westernized than the general masses, so much so that we can see socioeconomic differences between what we call *burgis* (elite) and *bakya* (mass) culture. (The term *bakya* comes from the footwear used by common Filipinos back in the day.) Much of Westernized Filipino culture is, more plainly, Americanized. American cultural attitudes, expressed mainly through glamorous Hollywood mythology or entertaining discourses on social media, have become part of our collective consciousness. Attitudes surrounding romance, fashion, ambition, and masculinity can be seen in the way we act and speak. Is a person, then, truly Filipino if their cultural leanings prioritize Western (that is, Euro-American) attitudes?

No amount of applied ethnic aesthetic can de-Westernize a person, for as the old saying goes, *Damitan mo man ang unggoy, unggoy pa rin.* (No matter how much you dress a monkey up, they are still a monkey.)

It comes across as inauthentic primarily because these aesthetics are worn as a costume over a Westernized interior. It is tokenism, or worse, appropriation. We know that there is a difference between appreciation and appropriation, and merely having Filipino citizenship does not necessarily mean that one understands the culture. Appreciation of a culture requires critical discernment of what is and is not true—in a polarizing political landscape, strong nationalism can be influenced by feel-good patriotic disinformation. Amidst all this, cultural expression must come from within for it to be a truly lived experience. So, again, immersion and education are vital in shaping authentic identity. Welcoming a variety of cultural expressions across the archipelago and around the globe allows us to weave that magnificent tapestry of shared heritage.

The Pure Filipino

In our search for culture, we might look for what makes a certain cultural identity the way it is. It is an insult to say that someone has no culture. But there is no single atom of pure culture that clearly distinguishes one from another. Things are borrowed, influenced, taken, or shared. Each element of a table is not the table itself. The table is the meaning we give to the pattern that emerges from these elements. In the same way, culture is not defined by only one aspect of it. It is easy to create stereotypes about certain cultures, but that is like saying that a table is only meant for dining. The table takes many forms and can be useful in many ways. Eventually, the wood of the table may rot, and its metal may rust. Although it has changed through time, it is still the same table, and memories have been created through it. Each scratch and stain holds a story. Culture is the same way.

Beyond the practical definition provided by the Philippine Constitution, it can be difficult to meaningfully and comprehensively define what it means to be Filipino. Defining it comes from an understanding of context. There are millions of us around the world. This then implies the transformation of the term itself, as well as its practical application in a globalized world. Loving adobo and being good at karaoke are surface-level stereotypes that do not guarantee cultural competence; they are not prerequisites to being part of the culture. Distinctions between urban and rural, local and diaspora, should not necessarily imply that one is more "authentic" than the other—rather, what these differences imply is that culture can be expressed in a myriad of wonderful ways.

CHAPTER THREE

-

Cultural Dialogue

As we discuss the various wondrous nuances of cultural aesthetics and the sociohistorical influences of personal identity, it is just as important to recognize the underlying mental frameworks we use in our judgments. These frameworks do not necessarily have any specific cultural baggage. I would say these frameworks are natural human tendencies: the inclination to prioritize oneself and one's immediate community. Ethnocentrism is an elevated echo of our biological need for self-preservation—of course, we want our family and peers to survive, because that would mean continued access to different kinds of resources. However, the dangerous extreme of this natural tendency is that we tend to judge outsiders based on our own standards, neglecting the potential for cross-cultural dialogue and mutually beneficial cultural trade.

Eventually, we might impose, as the colonizers did, our own ways of knowing onto other populations, who have their own ways of dealing with the elements of their native physical environments. There is so much learning and mutual flourishing that can happen when we participate in cross-cultural dialogue, but we tend to prefer the comfortable limitations of our own ethnicities and think ourselves better than others only because we know our ways best. If, as worldly travelers, we learned of better ways to live from elsewhere, we could adopt and adapt the best practices of various cultures, each one being a unique source of wisdom. This is the dream of a cross-indigenous psychology. To get there, however, we must challenge our ethnocentric and, on a more personal level, ego-tistic tendencies.

Cultural Hierarchies

In cultural studies, a particular culture sets the standard. This is why, in mid-century scholarship within the social sciences, we often read dis-cussions about "primitive" culture. Anglocentric social scientists looked at their own culture as the pinnacle of civilization, and they were often excited to study the faraway tribes in foreign jungles and islands because it afforded them the privilege of supposedly seeing the cultural develop-ment of man. Even in the work of the great psychologist Carl Jung, whose influence in the history of psychological thought we see in the study of archetypes, we can observe the tendency to find the "modern man" placed on the more developed end of cultural evolution. There is also unques-tionable romanticization of the exotic in Jung's work, where he often talks about the uninhibited and intuitive symbolic thinking of the prim-itive, in contrast to the neurotic repression of modern man. As Farhad Dalal pointed out, Jung explicitly engaged in stereotypical comparisons between European and African races.[1] It is important to recognize these tendencies, even in ourselves, when we engage in one-sided discussions of culture. All that said, Jung's suggestion is clear: We must embrace the wisdom of the ancient and mythic, which is still present today in film, literature, social customs, and dreams.[2] In doing so, we can integrate the intuitive symbolic realities that hold so much influence in our waking lives. I agree with this conclusion—our modern comforts come with new censorship, and the psycho-mystical realities that were once immediately accessible to our ancestors are now suppressed as "pagan," "superstitious," or even "demonic."

This deep irony can be seen in what Filipino priest-psychologist Father Jaime Bulatao called "split-level Christianity," where indigenous or folk reality lies buried but alive underneath a superficial and performative facade of Western morality.[3] Imagine, for example, a group of high school students in a Catholic school making dirty jokes in the hallway. A priest passes by and is immediately recognized by his outfit. The boys stop joking around and go over to ask for the priest's blessing. But once he leaves, they continue making foul jokes. This is Bulatao's split-level theory at work. Another example is when we pass by a church and make the sign of the cross, then later ask for the spirits' permission to cross a garden—in this case, two beliefs exist together, without offending each other. Bulatao said that this split-level tendency shows our need to appease the standards of Western authority while still living out our folk realities. Ma. Crisanta Nelmida-Flores pointed out that this way of thinking in the local social sciences encourages a dichotomy between urban and rural, of the "educated Christian elite" and the "uneducated, pagan, fanatical masses."[4] We see this a lot in the work of other pioneering social scientists who had to contend with the fact that there truly is a difference between the globalized worldview of our Westernized urban centers and the persistent animism of the idyllic countryside. In the field of folklore studies, reputable folklorists such as the great Father Francisco Demetrio point out that much of what we do know about pre-Hispanic beliefs can be found in the existing beliefs of modern-day animists.[5] These are, of course, drawn from ethnographic studies with our Indigenous communities. It is difficult to deny the ease with which we can gather anthropological information from Indigenous communities, especially since their living wisdom, passed on through generations, has somehow resisted the full influence of colonial ideologies. That is not to say that they have remained totally uninfluenced; we see that many Indigenous communities have been Christianized, yet somehow they retain their traditional aesthetics.

The affluent urbanite who looks for "authentic" culture might homogenize Indigenous communities to form what they think is the purely Filipino aesthetic, imagining that we all wore *bahag* (loincloth) and sported intricate tattoos. But this dilutes cultural nuance and says more about the desire of "modern man" to escape the chronically oppressive ennui of their modern comforts. It is possible to encourage authenticity through cultural exchange if only we resist the superstition that there is somehow a hierarchy of cultural purity.

Hierarchies in Society

We see the hierarchical mindset so well-manifested and unquestioned in our culture. "Going up the ladder" in order to "get to the top" follows the notion of succeeding by one's own hard work and merit (that is, meritocracy). This promotes ambition and competition, and, very often, exploitation and oppression. Related idioms are violent too: it is a "dog-eat-dog" world; building a career is a "rat race." We know, sadly, that most political and economic systems are built by a particular group of people for their own kind, effectively marginalizing everyone else. This is beyond our control; we know that some things are just easier for folks with a particular cultural identity and social class by their design. Meanwhile, the idea that we all start from somewhere is so pervasive that it is rarely questioned—yet why is it that we find it so impressive when someone from below the poverty line reaches an achievement such as graduating from school? Rags-to-riches stories are so impressive precisely because they are so rare, with failure being the common rule. But we all participate in the system of production and consumption, finding our value only in our ability to produce profitable material and consume the right things (for example, luxurious and trendy things). We believe that in participating in this cycle, we are gaining and maintaining our status, which gives us more access to resources. Our fear of losing status is what philosopher Alain de Botton called status anxiety. While the hunger for status can push us toward excellence, it also relies so much on so many things that are out of our control: global crises, historical faults and misfortunes, and harmful myths of the immorality of poverty.[6] Those who do not have status are considered "nobodies." Invisible, marginalized, and morally outcast.

We have negative connotations about those at the "bottom" as passive and submissive—meanwhile, those at the "top" are considered unique and remarkable. Beyond the practicality of salary grades, social status, and academic achievement, we also assume natural hierarchies such as those of age (that it is a proper and consistent indicator of wisdom) and tenure (just because a person has done something for a long time, their way is always correct). We also have symbolic hierarchies, such as "north" and "south." The north is associated with success ("nowhere to go but up") and knowledge ("north star"). The south, on the other hand, is associated with depression ("I feel down") and unfortunate events ("things are going south"). So, when we draw maps, those in the global north are considered more civilized—they are "on top." Meanwhile, those in the global south are thought of as lesser. Historically speaking, a large percentage of colonizers come from this global north. This mindset of superiority and inferiority has infected spirituality as well. We talk of a "higher self." God himself is a "man in the sky," while the devil and the damned live below, under the world. A 1943 drawing by Uruguayan artist Joaquín Torres García, titled *América Invertada*, depicts the farthest point of South America on top. These upside-down maps are seen as political statements, yet practically speaking, they are as correct as any ordinary map. Some maps portray northern and predominately white countries as bigger than others. This could be understood as the flattened distortion of a globe, but it may as well be a form of subtle racism. In any case, seeing different maps can challenge our north-based bias.[7]

"To Each Their Own" MINDSET

Hierarchies prioritize the individual over others. Hierarchies make sense because we want to live in relative comfort, and we want to ensure that we will always have access to resources. We know that we cannot trust other people to take care of us all the time, so many of us prefer doing things ourselves. After all, we cannot rely on others, but we can rely on ourselves. We can control our own actions, and if we are skilled enough, we can control the actions of others. We can call this philosophy *kani-ya-kaniya,* or "to each their own." It promotes extreme individualism. In our culture, we call those who carry this attitude *pilosopo,* which comes from the word *philosopher.* However, unlike the classical philosophers who taught us how to enhance our lives through the methodical application of reason, the pilosopo uses their intellect to enhance their own lives at the expense of others.

The pilosopo attitude is common among stubborn children, especially those who are starting to learn about their personal agency. This is an exciting time for children, but a frustrating time for parents. Imagine a parent telling their child to stop eating candies in their bed, to avoid attracting ants, but later they find their child on their bed eating chips. When the parent gets mad at the child, the child replies, "You told me to stop eating *candies* in bed—you said nothing about *chips!*" This juvenile example demonstrates how the pilosopo can be intentionally out of touch with appropriate context as a way to maintain their own comforts. Pilosopo are undeniably great at taking things apart, but they are often unwilling to consider how things come together. They are also talented at *lusot,* which is when something enters a narrow space, usually against all odds. Lusot is when someone slips through a closing door, or when someone avoids the ire of an irate authority figure by relying on their charisma. The pilosopo can definitely be charming: They are usually very good with words and are often incredibly astute. They are almost always technically correct; this is how they avoid negative consequences over and over again—most likely by causing linguistic frustration to whoever caught them red-handed. But in the most important moments, when their skills are needed by the collective, they often prioritize themselves. The pilosopo cares mainly about themselves; if they can get out of doing something tedious, they will. If they want something, they will find ways to get it, even if it is at the expense of others. When confronted with intuitive realities, they will bring up overly rational, out-of-touch solutions.

They embody the saying, *Kung ayaw may dahilan, kung gusto palaging merong paraan.* (If one does not want to do something, there are so many reasons, but if they want to do it, there are many available methods.)

We can argue endlessly about the ethics of any situation—anything can be argued to the point of making it useless. When talking about protecting the rights of a certain oppressed group, the pilosopo might say, "Why not protect the rights of *all* groups? Are we not all oppressed in our own way?" Of course, they are technically correct, but they also intentionally ignore the truth that certain groups are more oppressed than others simply because systems are built by those in power to maintain their own power. Pay attention whenever a societal process or structure is inconvenient or dangerous to someone—this often shows who this system is made for, and who it ignores.

In a way, the pilosopo encourages the status quo, especially if it is beneficial to them. The pilosopo's worldview is fundamentally kaniya-kaniya. This worldview is linear and hierarchical. The kaniya-kaniya mindset sees individuals as distinct entities, and in a world with limited resources, other people are competition. So, the pilosopo hoards resources to ensure their comfort—this, unfortunately, leads to a lot of waste, because one person's appetite can be satisfied with just enough. Anything more is overindulgence and will just rot in storage.

Those with the most resources are placed at the top of the hierarchy, and this higher status allows them to access even more resources. Ambition is the greatest value in a society that operates in a cycle of production and consumption. Here, we say that "money makes the world go around." A common metaphor for a person's career is a mountain that they must climb; to be successful is to be at the metaphorical peak. We do not want to be found at "rock bottom." Hierarchies imply domination, and historically, this is defined through destruction and ownership. The societies with more military force are somehow seen as more "civilized."

To the pilosopo, you only have yourself to blame for anything that happens to you. They believe that anything can be achieved if you set your mind to it—implying, therefore, that failure and poverty are entirely a person's fault alone. There is no mention of existing social systems that were built to work better for people who look and act a certain way, or for people who come from particular backgrounds deemed "right." In the kaniya-kaniya worldview, we are judged equally, but outside of context.

Frankly, the kaniya-kaniya worldview has given us our modern comforts through technological efficiency. It has also led to transactional relationships, feelings of isolation, and a loss of meaning in the face of a magnificent and terrifying universe. This is the dominant worldview, what we consider universal. It is the implicit dogma of societies that insist on individual greatness. It is an ever-expanding ego trip. The self becomes bigger and bigger, absorbing everything else. After the domination of nature and the domestication of animals, the kaniya-kaniya worldview leads to the colonization of other cultures.

Figure 3.1. *Kanlyak-Kanlya* mindset versus the *Tayo* mindset

Existential Hierarchies

On an existential level, the kaniya-kaniya worldview sees time as strictly linear. This is one way it affirms the cycle of production and consumption. If time is linear and one-way, then it must not be wasted. As a valuable commodity, it is "gold" that must be "spent wisely." Things—even those that are intangible, like time—are only valuable if they are useful (that is, profitable), so we say that we must "make the most of it." Our society is a clock-bound one, and we have set schedules, in the same way children draw lines in the sand to protect their sandcastles from an oncoming wave. We structure our days because we can better manage uncertainty if we set the parameters of what we can control. The pilosopo understands that anything that is "real" must also be measurable (so that, later, it can be manipulated or sold). The elements of the universe are believed to be static and reliable, and everything in it can be reduced to distinct qualities. As I said, this way of thinking has given us all our wonderful technological advancements. It has also removed us from our contextual relationship with the world.

Spiritually, this manifests in our suspicion of reality itself—many people think that the world might just be a simulation created by higher beings. The goal of modern spirituality seems to operate with the principles of kaniya-kaniya as well, especially in our obsession with becoming our "highest self," implying, therefore, a moral hierarchy. We want to reach "higher consciousness" by actualizing our best selves. Some of us believe that other people are not real; they are soulless programs that exist only to teach our cosmic soul some very important lessons. This solipsistic view of the world expresses a main character syndrome, a conceptualization of reality where we want to be the best, the most ascended, and the most morally conscious. It becomes performative—and, ironically, more ego-based. The Buddhist psychiatrist Mark Epstein pointed out that in our desire to expand our ego and become "one" with the universe, we really just end up identifying with an even larger ego. In this way, we are regressing to the helpless narcissism of our infancy, when we were one with the providence of our primary caregiver.[8] This is, unfortunately, a juvenile, self-centered spirituality. This tendency, however, has potential: We *can* become one with others, but only when we let go of the pretensions of the ego-driven "self."

Self and Identity

The word we use to refer to the self is *sarili,* which implies agency and ownership.[9] When we are keeping our body healthy, we say, *"Iniingatan ang sarili"* (taking care of the self). When we prioritize our well-being, we say, *"Paghahalaga sa sarili"* (valuing the self) or *"Pagmamahal sa sarili"* (loving the self). Confidence in one's ability in the face of uncertainty is called *Tiwala sa sarili* (trust in oneself). *Sarili* can also imply ownership, such as *Sariling pera* (one's money) or *Sariling bayan* (one's country). A person who has gone insane, or has momentarily deviated from their ordinary behavior, is said to have lost themselves—we say *"Nawala sa sarili,"* which means they wandered away from their sarili, as though the sarili is a defined center.

A person who only cares about their self is called *makasarili.* The prefix *maka-* is often used when one advocates for something. A nationalist is *maka-bayan,* a religious person is *maka-diyos,* and one who prioritizes their own comfort and security is makasarili. They may exploit people or hoard resources at the expense of others. That said, *sarili* does not necessarily refer to selfishness alone; it is one's sense of self when placed in context.

Leonardo Mercado has pointed out that within the concept of sarili, one can also find other concepts, such as loob (interiority) and *bait* (reason). Loob, meaning "inside," is a spatial metaphor for the inner world of affect, morality, and ambition. Much has been said about this concept because it appears so frequently in our language, and simply observing the way it is used implies much about the psychology of social dynamics. One's loob is recognized in one's interaction with others.[10] Charitable acts imply a beautiful loob *(kagandahang-loob)*, while someone with an ulterior motive has an evil interior *(masamang loob)*. The motivation to act emerges from within *(kusang loob)*, and the opening of one's interior *(bukas-loob)* corresponds to the opening of the palm *(bukas-palad)* as a way to mutually give and receive. One's loob is inwardly aware of social realities *(abot-malay)* and it feels with others as a form of solidarity *(abot-dama)*. Real change starts from within *(pagbabagong-loob)*, and when the individual is filled with conviction, their loob is complete *(buo ang loob)*.

Bait refers to one's sanity, but it is also the same word used to refer to one's goodness. A kind person is *mabait*. Forgetting oneself and going mad are the same; when one's bait breaks *(nasiraan ng bait)*, perhaps due to it being overwhelmed, the person becomes feral or unreasonable. Whereas in English the word *sanity* is generally understood to be just a person's ability to reason, *bait* is more holistic in that it recognizes one's ability to empathize with others and engage with common sense.

I would like to add a third dimension to the notion of the self: *alaala* (memory). In *Karunungan ng Dios*, a classic manuscript familiar to local esoteric practitioners, occultist Melencio T. Sabino laid out a mythology of Christianized animism. It is said that the Holy Trinity (Tatlong Persona) emerged from the sweat of the first god (Infinito Dios). Believing that they were the first to exist, they sat on three rocks, called Bait, Loob, and Alaala. Interestingly, these psychological terms appear in folk religious mythology, offering an intuitive structure of the psyche. Whereas bait refers to one's reasonableness and loob refers to the spectrum of one's subjective experience, alaala can refer to the markers of one's identity. Remembering something is *natandaan*, from the word *tanda*, meaning "mark" (that is, memory as a marker of past events). The process of aging is referred to as *pagtanda*, a word that also refers to the act of remembering. *Matanda* refers to an old person, one who is perhaps filled

Figure 3.2. Example *anting-anting* depicting the Thrones
of the Holy Trinity: Balt, Loob, and Alaala

with memory. The prefix *ma-* implies that a person has a large amount of
something, such as when one has a lot of *balahibo* or hair *(mabalahibo)*.
We might also say that a person who has a lot of appetite *(katakawan)* is
matakaw, or that a person has a lot of strength (*ma + lakas,* strength).
This is a way to describe the dominant trait of something, as when something is colorful (*ma + kulay,* color) or plain white (*ma + puti,* white).
One who is old is filled with the marks of memory (*ma + tanda,* mark).
Alaala, then, is one's collected experience, from which we can fully define
sarili.[11] The Thrones of the Holy Trinity are the three vital psychological
aspects of the human mind.

The fullness of sarili is in letting go of it, not in the sense that it is
totally forgotten, but rather that it is transcended as to merge with

collective consciousness. Losing one's identity *(nawala sa sarili)* is to be thrown into disarray. On the other hand, it is the strengthening of one's identity that allows one to let go of it, precisely because this identity is no longer limited to one's individuality. Bulatao observed that the heroes of our history have been those who have gone beyond the limitations of the self, expanding their scope of identity to include community and country.[12] The realization of individual potential does not necessarily follow a hierarchy or checklist of needs; it is simply when the liberation and stability of *tayo* (together) are considered as essential to the survival of sarili.

Cross-Indigenous Interaction

Let us now consider an alternative worldview to the kaniya-kaniya, which we can refer to as the *tayo* mindset. The tayo prioritizes the sustainability of resources over the eradication of competition—that is, collaboration over competition. There are no hierarchies in tayo: responsibility is shared. We can practice this by engaging with cultures beyond our own. We see and appreciate that there are ways of knowing and living that may contradict our beliefs, but they may also improve on them. By being open to this, we ground ourselves in a collective consciousness.

In indigenous psychology, the preferred approach when engaging with foreign cultures is to view them as sources of wisdom, not targets of analysis. When we let people come from their own perspectives and contribute their own ways of knowing, we engage in cross-indigenous or kros-katutubo discourse.[13] Although this approach is used mainly in indigenous research, it is not something that only academics can do—we are encouraged to do this in our everyday lives as an antidote to egotism and ethnocentrism.

As a guide, let us look at the basic principles of indigenous methods. Whenever I refer to "researchers" here, I also mean anyone who intends to visit a place to learn about its culture. In a monograph published by the national association for Sikolohiyang Pilipino, Rogelia Pe-Pua discussed five, as follows:[14]

First, the quality of information we can gather from our study relies on the depth of relationship between researcher and informant. Treating them appropriately as kapwa (fellow man) encourages the kind of insight we get from good friends. When we meet new cultures, the best attitude is one of *pakapa-kapa* or groping in the dark. Drop all universal ideas you may have and engage with new customs as they are. Ask questions without imposing your own standards and impressions. Be curious. If, in your dialogue, they ask about your own culture, it is an invitation for you to share your own wisdom. Be open to this, as we must sometimes give to receive. This attitude is bukas-palad, an open palm, ready to do charitable action and accept blessings.

Second, the researcher and informant must honor the fact that they are equals. The informants are not guinea pigs to be exploited. In the academic research standards set by Western institutions, we might collect data by isolating individuals from their natural environments—even today, a good informant interview might involve a "neutral" meeting place. But indigenous methods encourage the researcher to go into the informants' area and to participate in their customs and, if possible, immerse themselves in the culture by living in it with the community. The researcher should accept a certain level of social responsibility in that context *(panunuluyan)*. If it is safe to do this, it is much better to speak from the position of experience rather than of assumption.

Third, the informants' well-being must be prioritized over the data that would be gathered. It is the duty of the researcher to learn more, but if releasing information (for example, sacred traditions or taboo practices) would come at the cost of the community's livelihood and safety, it is best to indefinitely delay the project. If a communal need presents itself during the course of the research, the researcher has an ethical responsibility to address that need.

Fourth, the researcher must be sensitive to the needs of the informants, so they know the best methods to use. Sensitivity to verbal and nonverbal social cues is called *pakikiramdam,* a form of social empathy. It is like "reading the room," but that connotes effort. Pakikiramdam is intuitive and effortless—all it requires is social mindfulness. We should not be frustrated that social norms are unsaid, especially if we are the ones who are entering the space. The rude tourist, or shall I say, the intruder, might be committing multiple social sins when they visit local sites: They tend to be loud, arrogant, and inconsiderate. They mess with sacred sites and cut corners. The intruder treats exotic locales as theme parks. But these places are home to many people; meaning and history are embedded in these special areas. The cosmopolitan travels to experience worlds beyond their own; unlike the intruder, the cosmopolitan does not seek to escape the tedium of their own culture, but rather they seek to enhance it by learning from other cultures. The cosmopolitan has conversations with locals; they eat and act as locals do. They are true adventurers. The researcher with pakikiramdam participates in this great adventure: to experience a place as the people there do. Whereas the intruder only takes pictures and collects aesthetics, the cosmopolitan makes memories and gifts.

Fifth, whenever possible, the researcher must speak in the local language. Language is the way we share ideas, values, and attitudes. If the researcher cannot learn the language due to a lack of time, they must find someone who can translate for them. This practice is called finding a *tulay* (bridge). The tulay is a person who is part of that community, who can introduce you to the culture and ease the potential tension between you and the locals. It is easier for us to trust someone who is also trusted by someone familiar to us. Collaborating with a tulay can allow researchers and cosmopolitans to better participate in the local customs.

In the end, the point is to see through systems and to finally find ourselves as part of a larger thing. To treat people as equals: not merely as extensions of ourselves but as varied manifestations of what it means to be human. Although these principles were developed primarily for researchers, we can use them too in our everyday lives.

CHAPTER FOUR

-

Learning and Unlearning

My father taught me that school is just a place where you learn how to learn. Practical matters involving the specifics of your daily duties and professional life after graduation can be learned when the time comes. School is where you develop important tools for intellectual and social resiliency. It is where you sharpen your critical thinking and practice ways of knowing and communicating. These are skills that are necessary for surviving in a shared world. On the most basic level, a good educational institution's task is to pass on the knowledge of what has worked for human beings in the past—as well as what has not worked—in a timely and culturally accessible manner. However, rather than saying, "This is what has worked for us," the system has been saying, "This is how the world works." There is a finality in this proclamation. It is like saying, "Think this way and act this way, or else."

On the most basic, personal level, what we call "decolonization" is just a process of unlearning. That is, the dropping of unhelpful frameworks and assumptions to allow for the flourishing of native understanding. "Native" here only refers to that which naturally grows from the cultural ground. In other words, "native understanding" could mean whatever is most resonant and helpful to you in your particular context. Just because it is indigenous to a certain place does not make it useful or liberating. We cannot simply assume that anything indigenous is good, and everything Western is bad—these are reductive essentialisms that ignore the dynamism of worldviews as cultures continue to interact with other cultures and their own transforming environments. Many Western ways of thinking are very much aligned with the ambitions of indigenization movements, such as intersectionality and feminism. In fact, it would seem that many indigenization and liberatory movements around the world are aligned in various ways. For example, in reading a fantastic article on African psychology by Stephen Baffour Adjei, I was struck by how similar our indigenous psychologies are.[1] Our nuanced conceptions of personhood are aligned in that they are perceived as inherently relational. Although our written histories are different, the struggles are very familiar. As you continue to read this book, understand that this is not only Filipino—it is, more importantly, human.

So, I echo the call of Sylvia Estrada Claudio, who said that indigenous psychology should go beyond nationalist and reductionist views of culture.[2] Within our culture there are already so many different experiences, so much so that the burgis (elite) and bakya (masses) have little in common, except being called "Filipino." One's values and beliefs depend on what a person has access to, based on their social location— that is, their gender, family, socioeconomic class, religious affiliation, ethnolinguistic group, and so on. There are also differences between how culture is expressed locally and in the diaspora, and although I have had many fascinating conversations with Filipinos who moved abroad, or were born and raised in other countries, I cannot claim to fully empathize with their challenges as immigrants or members of a minority group—most of which I do not have to face, being at home in the Philippines. What we can hope for, then, is a cross-indigenous approach, which gives everyone a seat at the table. Again, I would never wish to impose my way of thinking—all I could ever hope for is that these concepts and frameworks help us find a common psychological (and maybe even spiritual) language to add to our growing toolkit of liberatory thought.

Unlearning is not fantasizing, in that we might dream of possibilities so removed from reality, restructure shared truths to match our standards, and ignore difficult and contradictory realities, only because we want certain falsehoods to be real. Unlearning means reconnecting with what is true, precisely by challenging these fantasies—and, in our case, this refers to the many cultural myths, lies, and stereotypes that we have learned through political or ethnocentric propaganda in school, social media, and the larger society.

Ways of Knowing

Let us look into two ways we can learn more about culture. The first is academic, and the other is immersive. One is not better than the other, and both certainly have their pros and cons. The academic approach encourages participation in the larger scholarly discourse of great thinkers who have digested the varieties of cultural expression to present them with renewed clarity. Good, accessible research that is easy to read is a form of literary telepathy. The more we read and consume relevant media, the more perspectives we are exposed to, and like a well-balanced meal, what we choose to take in can nourish us. Still, it often solidifies intellectual biases as "truth," especially if this work becomes foundational reading for future scholars. The reader might mistake book knowledge for experience, in the same way that a tourist might say that they have experienced a foreign country, having only read a travel book.

On the other hand, the immersive approach encourages full first-hand exposure. This is not merely sitting and watching; this is getting involved. At least for the duration of their stay, the researcher becomes a part of the culture, joining their customs and accepting communal responsibilities. The researcher learns what it means, not only aesthetically, but also personally—one can always describe experiences, but assessing the quality of food based on a restaurant review is very different from fully tasting the flavors of a meal. However, immersion limits the researcher to a particular culture, and this may create in-group biases in their thinking. Furthermore, their intrusion may be initially treated with politeness, but like any house guest, they may eventually become a nuisance. Without the right training, openness, and connections within the community, the researcher may be imposing themselves onto the locals, offending them with social taboos that they were not even aware of. We do not often bring up the rudeness of strangers, except among each other, but these subtle feelings can create tension and distance.

Whichever approach you decide on is up to you, so long as you feel that you are equipped to handle the nuances of your chosen field. I will now discuss concrete ways through which we can apply these approaches in the study of identity, culture, and indigenous psychology.

THE ACADEMIC APPROACH

Zeus Salazar said that there are four ways through which folk psychology has been studied in the history of the Philippine social sciences. These "four filiations" are the academic-scientific, academic-philosophical, ethnic, and psycho-medical.[3] The first approach, academic-scientific, is guided by the pragmatic and behaviorist approach of American psychology. It may rely more on experimentation and statistics. The academic-philosophical approach draws from the theological training in Catholic universities, particularly through the Jesuit tradition and the philosophy of Saint Thomas Aquinas. Salazar pointed out that this approach involves "pre-scientific" reflections on the native worldview. The ethnic, or katutubo, approach draws primarily from the language, customs, and literature of the people. This is the basis of our modern indigenization movements. The common sense psychology of the people that grew naturally from their lived experience—this is called *kinagisnang sikolohiya*. From this, we can find patterns and appropriate, inclusive frameworks that encapsulate a more general experience.

Outsider researchers can also do ethnic psychology on certain cultures, but their reading might only consider that which is surface level. We know that everyday cultural experiences are much deeper than what is merely observable, and social dynamics are more nuanced, complicated, and context-based. In academic research, we call this the etic approach, which is assumed to be objective and bias-free, but it is still somewhat biased—from the perspective of the researcher's own culture. It is great that the etic approach allows insiders to see what may not already be obvious, but the uniqueness of one culture is inevitably going to be more apparent from the perspective of another culture. Nevertheless, this is the foundation of early anthropological research, from which, today, we learn about who we used to be—but we must acknowledge that this was written through their eyes, which were not always kind, and were almost always willing to promote imperialist propaganda.

For example, ancient practices such as crossing genders in religious practice or same-sex romantic partnership may have seemed incredibly unusual to outsiders who lived with more binary gendered norms and particular customs around sexuality. This may be one reason why the old European chroniclers found it so important to record certain instances of what they perceived to be barbarism—precisely because they were so different from what they were used to. As Tom Sykes points out in *Imagining Manila,* early colonial literature shifted depending on prevailing attitudes, often promoting the colonizer as a peacekeeper or bringer of civilization and debasing the exotic natives as brutal and primitive savages desperately in need of education, sanitation, and economic liberation.[4] These promises were, of course, underdelivered, if at all. In any case, the outsider's perspective is almost always comparative, or what Salazar called *pansila*—that is, "for-them."[5] The outsider's culture is used as a point of reference to study different cultures, and it becomes the standard, while the other becomes the target of analysis and historiography.

The insider's approach, called emic, comes from what is already known. It is understood in ways aligned with existing social dynamics.

The insider knows their worldview better than the outsider, and so they are considered a "culture-bearer." Here, we must critically examine assumptions about knowledge that is said to be "universally true." Rather than impose outsider standards, the insider looks inward. Local indigenous research looks at kapwa with eyes that know and understand what it is like to be kapwa, challenging the distant and extractive methods of outsider research. That is not to say that the outsider can never understand—as we already know, the outsider can become an insider by feeling with others (pakikiramdam) and participating in the culture. In this way, *ibang tao* (outsider) becomes *hindi ibang tao* (one of us). This may, in the end, be a more enriching approach, as the researcher has their feet rooted in two different grounds, becoming one with all.

The fourth filiation, according to Salazar, is the psycho-medical, and this involves the study of local spirituality and healing frameworks, with the assumption that the modern practices of the folk healer draw from an undercurrent of folk tradition that comes from the precolonial. While much of it has been Christianized, it is obvious that the old worldviews persist. Resil Mojares used the term *Christianized animism* to refer to these practices, mainly because they are not simply localizations of Christian practice, but rather more ancient traditions that have simply appropriated Christian symbolism.[6]

THE IMMERSIVE APPROACH

As an academic, I was trained with research methods that can be extractive and exploitative. We were taught to isolate subjects in order to collect data—in a sterile laboratory or, for interviews, in secure, secret spaces where they could feel comfortable opening up. For many of us, however, it is more uncomfortable to open up when we are taken out of our natural environment. When we are brought to a new space, we do not know its unique dangers. All this time, the approach of scientific research has been to remove things from their context to study their features and functions independently. For the most part, the social sciences tend to do the same thing, wherein informants who are going to share deeply personal, traumatic, or culturally protected knowledge are often invited to offices or cafés, where they are interviewed—or, as it usually feels, interrogated. In this approach, the researcher might believe that the most important thing is to assess the quality of the questions they would ask so that they could gather the right kind of information. In academic institutions, research proposals often include an appendix with the questions to be asked, for the assessment and approval of their superiors. Ethical standards insist that informants are made to sign waivers and long consent forms, which essentially say that they approve that whatever they say can and will be used in analysis and information dissemination. In the end, the one who benefits, in terms of recognition and additional funding, is almost always the researcher, their institutional affiliation, and their sponsors. Meanwhile, the informants are left to go back to their lives. If they are lucky, some policymaker gets to read the research and implement life-saving interventions for the community. This is rarely the case, but we can still hope. Otherwise, a businessperson might find the research and use it as an opportunity to create a product that fills a gap illuminated by the research, successfully capitalizing on the actual needs of real people.

The reason many communities protect each other from outsiders is mainly that outsiders are not to be trusted: They often come in only to take, and many of them misinterpret the insiders' lived experiences for profit. I can think of expensive, whitewashed spiritual retreats based on indigenous religions, egocentric autoethnographies of a foreigner's journey to an exotic land, and for-profit neocolonial systems tokenizing indigenous experiences to expand their consumer base. Yet we also know that, without appropriate collaboration with outsiders, it can be incredibly difficult to preserve, popularize, and integrate many important aspects of our cultural heritage. Ethical nonextractive research can also lead to culture-appropriate policy changes. For so long, we have been relying on foreign norms and standards to model our social systems. Indigenous research allows us to come from our own experience and make educated judgments about what we need and what is useful.

Introduced in the previous chapter, we now revisit Rogelia Pe-Pua's 2005 monograph, which outlined the methodology of indigenous research.[7] The methods have been developed and used by many researchers for decades. I will describe some of them here, and although they were mainly offered to social scientists in the field, we can also apply them whenever we are called to learn more about a culture. First, the researcher enters by removing all assumptions of what is universal and approaches with a sense of curiosity. This is called pakapa-kapa, groping in the dark. They might then ask the locals questions *(pagtatanong-tanong)*, not in isolated environments but in the streets, in their homes, in the corner shop: wherever they already are. Considering the researcher's safety and the community's resources, they can stay with a household for a short time *(pakiki-panuluyan)* or a longer time *(paninirahan)*. In indigenous research, this may be more appropriate than staying at a hotel, as it encourages trust between the researcher and the community. So, the researcher can stay for longer, and if they become a contributing part of the household, this is called *pananahanan*.

The researcher does not have to go so far as to wear what the locals are wearing in an attempt to fit in. This might be perceived as mockery by the locals. The researcher should instead wear something comfortable and weather-appropriate. When asking questions, there may be topics that are initially awkward to discuss. If there is resistance or silence, this could mean that the relationship between the researcher and informants has not yet gone deep enough. In this case, the researcher should be open to diverting from a strict list of preapproved questions—instead, they should be able to find indirect ways to discuss these topics. This approach may extend to certain cultural traits that may be frowned upon, especially in the context of family or community values. Rather than the "hot seat" of an isolated interview, the researcher engages in *pakikipagkuwentuhan* or sharing stories. In other words, the researcher offers their own insight as a show of solidarity. They are not observers who are objective or outside. They are part of the space.

On the surface, it would seem many of these methods are already known to the social scientist—after all, all these immersive methods are just variations of participant observation, which is already being done. The main difference is the value placed on the relationship between researcher and informant. Indigenous research methods carry their own ethical considerations, but it is important to acknowledge their merit as alternatives to extractive methods. Because we are humans learning about other humans, it is vital that we recognize uneven power dynamics in the context of culture and history and actively practice our shared humanity. It is in the field of indigenous research that we see the direct application of kapwa (shared identity) and pakikiramdam. Whereas extractive research enters with an agenda and leaves once they have gotten what they need, indigenous research prioritizes the informants and their community. These ethical principles have already been discussed in the previous chapter, but this one may need repeating: the well-being of the community is more important than our desire to learn more about them.

My Own Education

My mother frequently and fondly recounts the story of my very first day of school, where the teacher asked the children to name an animal that they knew. Many of them said "dog" and "cat," and then I raised my hand and said, "orca!" I do not recall whether I was trying to impress anyone; all I remember from that time is that I had all these large, wonderful, and fully illustrated books of animals, planets, and dinosaurs. I am sure I found an orca in one of those books. I greatly enjoyed books with random facts about the world, and in my younger days, I would read almost anything. I have always been fascinated by mythology, particularly by wizards and mythical beasts. I wrote my own little books and visited magical worlds. Sadly, whenever I would be eager to share, the people around me would look at me funny. Once in class, I was excited to share my excitement over learning a very long word, *pneumonoultramicroscopicsilicovolcanoconiosis*, but I was met with silence and side eyes. My childhood imagination was seen as strange, and people would often comment that I lived in my own little world: *"May sariling mundo."* Often, this phrase implies that a person is living in a schizophrenic or hallucinatory reality.

Eventually, through numerous episodes of social embarrassment, I learned that there is a range of what people expect you to know at certain points in your life. Precociousness is not always welcome. Authorities do not want you to know more than they do, and will say that it is for your own good, and peers do not want you to go too far beyond what is comfortable for them. In my experience, a well-read person is not always well-received, usually because people do not want to feel stupid around them. The individualist might say that it is not their responsibility to make people feel intelligent, but I think that is an exclusionary approach to knowledge. If I feel excited about knowing something, I want others to know it as well. Reflecting on myself, I realize that it was not what I knew that was the problem; it was how I shared my knowledge. Perhaps I had been acting with the subconscious intention to impress others, to make it seem like what I know is incredible, which would in turn make *me* incredible. But what I knew was just book knowledge, facts that were interesting but useless, at least on a practical everyday level. Not long ago, I was told that the way I used to discuss things made it seem that I knew more than everyone else without considering what they already knew. I was, in effect, just monologuing.

The more I learned and practiced indigenous psychology, the more I understood that knowledge is a shared creation that comes from people rather than something imposed on them. I used to do my lectures as a straight spew of information, but I never stopped to consider whether my students truly understood what I was saying. When I would ask questions to the class, I would get frustrated when nobody would answer. I took it as their indifference, rather than my lack of skill in teaching.

Applying indigenous methods, I shifted my mindset from top-down (teacher-centered) to bottom-up (learner-oriented). Before carrying on with the discussion, I assess their existing knowledge about the topic (pakapa-kapa) and build from there. I encourage them to find applications in their everyday lives by sharing my own experiences with certain concepts and frameworks (pakikipagkuwentuhan). Being the teacher, I do have more expertise in my field of interest, but I try not to begin by imposing what I know and expecting everyone to "get on my level." We are building on information about a shared world; I am not some prophet from beyond who came to deliver news from the gods. So, I would have to bring them into the conversation by defining a common language (jargon) and a way of thinking (an epistemological framework). It is an invitation. I have always found it strange that there are teachers who pride themselves on being labeled a "terror," and teachers who boast about their low passing rate. If anything, this shows more about their lack of empathy and pedagogical skill. Some students are truly indifferent despite fantastic teachers, and some teachers are too lax, so the quality of education suffers. We can take our cue from studies within the field of positive psychology, which defines the ideal state of growth and creativity as the match between well-defined challenges and confidence in one's personal ability to face them.[8] In my own continued learning and unlearning, I have applied this principle. I would not take more than what I could handle, and I would not pretend to know more than I do. I would work within my capacity, expanding from there. Slowly but surely, this does make a difference.

My approach to learning blends academic research and immersive experience. I find academic perspectives that allow me to understand my lived experiences and I use realities from my personal life to affirm what I read. Frankly, it is easy for me to discard what I feel is dated or useless, as I always consider *when* something was written, and *for whom* it was written. At this point, I can often recognize whether a particular thinker does not resonate with the approach and insights of another simply by noticing whether they did not use the other's relevant work. For example, in a 2014 lecture on the tenth anniversary of the death of writer Nick Joaquin, Resil Mojares pointed out how many serious historians have not considered Joaquin's scholarly writings on culture and history—mainly because he was known for his fiction.[9] This is, Mojares said, an example of snobbery, perhaps because Joaquin wrote in such an easy-to-read and passionate way.

I can also notice whether a thinker has not fully understood another's work before launching into a heated polemic against them. Some points might have already been addressed in a paper that their subject of criticism has written. Commonly, we will not be able to read everything that a person writes, and even if we were able to do so, we would not fully know the nuance and dynamism of how they think. It is easy to argue with written texts because they cannot respond. A book is only alive while it is being written. In this sense, reading can be a form of necromancy, but it is only ever a glimpse, a message, a snapshot of an organic consciousness that moves through time and is transformed by experience. In any case, I find it all to be amusing gossip, and it reminds me that academics are still human—they can be kind and wise, but also reactive and misinformed. I do not want to get embroiled in these heated discourses myself, preferring rather to take what is useful and discard what is not, instead participating in an academic and literary buffet of ideas. That said, I do expect that there will be those who would disagree with me—what an exciting opportunity for mutually edifying discourse!

Propaganda and Anti-Intellectualism

I do sometimes consider myself an academic, mainly because that is what I do (teaching and research), but the term itself suggests an ivory tower, a fortress detached from the world. Anyone who participates in the systematic search for knowledge is, in some way, an academic in spirit, and must be encouraged to continue documenting the world through their active participation in it. I do hope for greater popularization of ideas that have been developed within academe, to challenge public misinformation and encourage nuanced thinking. Unfortunately, we see today a lot of anti-intellectualism—locally, when faced with someone who triggers our intellectual insecurities, we might say, in a very sarcastic tone, *"E di ikaw na ang matalino!"* (Fine, you are the smartest!) I feel like this comes from a misalignment between what we intuitively know through socialization and how we are taught through institutions. In the Philippines, good education is difficult to access and maintain, especially considering the state of poverty and the lack of budget to rehabilitate dilapidated and crowded schools. Consider also the many underpaid and overworked teachers, many of whom may move abroad to find better opportunities to financially support themselves and their families. We lose many skilled practitioners—teachers, doctors, engineers, and so on—when they seek better opportunities elsewhere because they have difficulty supporting themselves here. We call this "brain drain." These are the realities of our educational system: Many do not finish their schooling, and many more finish half-heartedly. In 2022, the World Bank reported severe "learning poverty" in the Philippines, where 91 percent of children around age ten have difficulty reading.[10]

Although reading can be a gateway to the world's knowledge, educational institutions must go farther. In their essay "The Mis-education of the Filipino," Renato Constantino called for an education that prioritizes the needs of the people and promotes an awareness of heritage and community.[11] I am nostalgic for publicly accessible television shows from the 1990s and early 2000s that were well-produced and educational. *Sine'skwela* (1994–2004) taught us about science and was aligned with the curriculum of public elementary school students. *Math-tinik* (1997–2004) taught children math; *Hiraya Manawari* (1995–2003) taught cultural and family-oriented values through folktales. I remember these shows fondly, and I learned much from them. I wonder how these might find equivalence today.

We know that educational institutions can be used as a tool for propaganda, and we have seen this in early colonial schools that promoted foreign values and inculcated a sense of cultural inferiority among us. Today, there is also political propaganda and historical distortion. In 2023, the Department of Education received a proposal to remove the name Marcos from "Diktadurang Marcos" (Marcos Dictatorship) in the elementary curriculum.[12] Many have called out this attempt to whitewash a very difficult time not so far in the past, a period in our history that has been criticized for its human rights abuses and widespread corruption. If we are to encourage true learning, we must be vigilant. Researchers do not have to be affiliated with institutions to be students of culture. Teachers, journalists, scientists, and all seekers of knowledge carry light in increasingly dark times, where it is easy to silence those who seek and speak the truth. They are our culture-bearers, and they have a responsibility to document, preserve, and facilitate the continued development of culture.

Still, this time is very exciting—there is a deeply fulfilling kind of pleasure that can be gained from knowing more, from seeing ordinary things in a new light, or even from deconstructing and destroying intellectual idols and false gods.

CHAPTER FIVE

Cultural Domination

The effects of colonization persist to this day—in existing political and economic systems as well as internalized beliefs of cultural inferiority. Attitudes associated with the affirmation and the promotion of colonial systems are called the "colonial mentality." In a 1994 monograph, Virgilio Enriquez identified six phases of cultural domination: denial and withdrawal, destruction and desecration, denigration and marginalization, redefinition and token utilization, transformation and mainstreaming, and commercialization and commodification.[1] We can simplify Enriquez's six phases into three: invalidation, destruction, and commodification. The process of cultural domination is known as *pananakop*, which refers to taking things without permission, to become part of one's scope, or *sakop*.

Indigenous culture is *invalidated* when it is set against foreign standards. It may, for example, be seen as "savage," "uncivilized," or "underdeveloped" compared to others. It also involves erasing language, mocking accents, marginalizing folk art and literature, and demonizing or denigrating spirituality as mere superstition. The *destruction* of culture occurs when artifacts and manuscripts are burned, sacred lands are desecrated, culture-bearers are persecuted, and natural resources are exploited and controlled. It also involves the denial of cultural dynamism as well as the impractical Westernization of systems. Cultural aesthetics, such as ethnic patterns and plant wisdom, may also be taken out of context and sold—so begins the *commodification* of indigenous culture. Today, many of us seek out cultural aesthetics to express them in our modern art and fashion. We must know what these aesthetics mean so we can represent them well—otherwise, we are only wearing a costume. When the foreigner forces the native to wear their clothes and speak their language, the native may do it well, but only to appease the outsider. In the same way, the foreigner may emulate the native's appearance without actually knowing what any of their special patterns mean. This is *pagpapanggap* (pretension), which is outward and shallow. Commodification also involves exoticizing indigenous spiritual practices and promoting the land and its people as hospitable and virginal, ready and willing to be conquered.

In this chapter, I will be using examples in Philippine culture and history to illustrate my points, but it is more important to understand the insidious underlying process. These examples are tangible but subtle manifestations of cultural domination; they may happen anywhere else, regardless of how they might occur in other societies.

Invalidation

Invalidation marginalizes culture, assuming that there is a center. When I was working with communities, I was encouraged to use the term *vulnerable* to refer to those integrated into the system who have difficulty adapting to it. In the case of cultural dominance, I think *marginalization* is more appropriate: we become the "other" in a system that was not primarily designed for us. We experience this when cultural expressions—physical, linguistic, spiritual, and artistic—are set aside in favor of some other ideal. Eventually, we internalize this otherness, and we begin to invalidate ourselves.

INVALIDATING APPEARANCE

As I sit in traffic along densely packed local roads, it is difficult to ignore the massive billboard advertisements featuring various whitening products—soaps, creams, pills, procedures, and more. Every other commercial on TV features ways to smoothen one's naturally curly hair or whiten one's skin in just seven days. As far as we know, many of the models and endorsers for these products are born with mixed genetic heritage, which we call *may lahi*. In other words, many of them are not fair-skinned because they use the products, but because they were born with fair skin, which seems—pardon my pun—unfair, at least in terms of honest advertising. The term *may lahi* almost always refers to having a lighter skin color, such as among the Chinito/Chinita (fair-skinned Asian) or Mestizo/Mestiza (Caucasian). There is another term, *mabango*, referring to something that smells good, that is used to refer to people who look fragrant—and this is usually observed through Westernized manifestations of wealth, status, appearance, and fashion. One who looks may lahi might also look mabango.

In mainstream media—especially in movies and *teleseryes* (soap operas), but also in beauty pageants and among online influencers—celebrated features include having an angular nose *(matangos)*, being tall *(matangkad)*, and, of course, being white *(maputi)*. We know, however, that, to the insecurity of many, most Philippine natives have a flat nose *(pango)*, an average height of five feet tall, and brown or dark skin *(moreno/morena)*. Even recently, blackface and brownface have been used to portray certain characters of different ethnolinguistic groups—even when an actor is naturally fair-skinned. This makes it easier for the story to visually show a character's transformation into someone who might be considered more beautiful—that is, whiter. So we see here that our current beauty standards are not only limited to the color of our skin, but to a pattern that is nonnative, at least if based on the general population.

Our word for beauty, *kagandahan,* does not only refer to physical appearance; it also refers to something good or sufficient.[2] When we want to wish someone a good day, we might say, *"Magandang araw po!"* Good news is called *magandang balita,* and a charitable act is *kagandahang-loob* (referring to a person's beautiful loob or interior). On the other hand, ugliness *(pangit)* also does not refer only to physical appearance; it also refers to what is morally undesirable. A bad attitude is *pangit na ugali,* a bad lifestyle is *pangit na pamumuhay*. We can therefore recognize what our society values by what we consider beautiful. It is easy, then, to conflate physical beauty with moral goodness, and if our standards of physical beauty are decidedly foreign, then we have to recognize whether our moral standards are foreign as well.

Ideally, everyday beauty products would enhance and maintain what is naturally there, not replace it with something totally different. The intentionality with which we are so willing to change our skin color, nose or eye shape, and even height says more about what is perceived to be attractive by society—not necessarily what we find truly attractive. It speaks of a fundamental insecurity ingrained in us: that the foreign appearance of whiteness signifies not only beauty but social status and physical prowess. This is even echoed in our belief in the mystical entities known as engkanto, which are usually described as tall, wealthy, attractive, and Caucasian, perhaps a supernatural manifestation of our former colonizers.[3] It is interesting to note also that the engkanto can be obsessive and vengeful—once they fall in love with a mortal, that person would disappear and then reappear in the wilderness, undressed and disheveled, with little memory of their kidnapping. In the Visayas, they are called *dili ingon nato*, which means "not like us." They are human, but not quite—something about them is a little strange or otherworldly, at least compared to what we are used to.

It would be interesting, then, to see what beauty and goodness might mean as it emerges naturally from our everyday experiences. This does not necessarily mean rejecting Eurocentric beauty standards, because we can set our own standards without bringing others down; nor does it mean only insisting on particular "native" features, because this may just be done out of a surface-level desire for aesthetic inclusion. It is, therefore, a balance of clear-eyed perception and openness to variations of beauty.

INVALIDATING LANGUAGE AND LITERATURE

When I was in elementary school, we were only allowed to speak in Filipino during August, which is the Buwan ng Wika, the national month of local languages. Whenever we would utter a Filipino word in class, we had to place one peso into the class fund—I never knew where these funds went, but they were supposed to make our classroom facilities better. My English teachers in high school never spoke in Filipino, and I remember that we would celebrate whenever they would break character in some way. When I was about to graduate high school, our English teacher promised that she would speak in Filipino as a graduation present, and on our final day, she said, *"Ano ba ang gusto ninyong sabihin ko?"* (What do you want me to say?) The class erupted in a deafening cheer. These little ridiculous anecdotes show the priorities of our educational system, at least in the way I experienced it.

There is nothing wrong with speaking and writing in English. Language is just the way we communicate with each other. But there is something to be said about the marginalization of local languages in our educational system. Insisting that we should teach only in Filipino may not be the best practice either; this nativistic attitude could isolate us from participation in shared global knowledge. But forcing the foreigner's English and actively pushing aside Filipino seems like a surface-level choice that may not be conducive to actual learning. Language is how we communicate vital information; it is also the way we subtly imbibe cultural values and ideologies. Discussing academic topics comfortably means using the most appropriate language. Thankfully, in conversation, we naturally blend English and Filipino, but academic purists would say that this only splits our consciousness. I do not think so. We express what is naturally within, and our choice of language is how we express it, with fair consideration to who we are speaking to.

The Filipino accent is also often the subject of ridicule. I see this a lot in comedy specials, where the comedian—sometimes even fellow Filipinos—would exaggeratedly use our native accents, often to cater to a foreign audience who find our accent unusual or exotic. I do not intend to be fascistic about the "right" type of comedy—I can laugh at myself and good ironic observations about my culture. Of course, funny voices can be used for comedic purposes, even to amuse children, but it is often obvious when an accent is used only because it sounds exotic, delivered to an audience encouraged to mock it. We have to acknowledge the reality that certain accents are generally considered to be "sophisticated" and "seductive," while others are supposedly said to sound "uneducated" or "sinister." In my undergraduate studies, I took French for a foreign language course because I thought it would be attractive—and not for any other reason. Today, I only remember how to say, "My name is ..." and "I am tired." I never used it again, but it was an amusing semester—mainly because our teacher only ever spoke to us in French.

Our literature is not only in Filipino—many, like me, also write in English. Sometimes they write in a combination of both for a more casual audience. Unfortunately, most local books are only published in limited numbers, so many wonderful texts have tragically gone out of print. To make matters more difficult, most popular bookstores only dedicate one section or shelf to all local publications, labeled "Filipiniana." The genres blend on the Filipiniana shelf: fiction and nonfiction share the same spot, but everywhere else in the bookstore, foreign books are categorized according to their theme and niche. Happily, most independent bookstores place local publications beside foreign ones if they are of the same category. To the extreme, the practice of setting Filipiniana aside can be a form of literary or academic oppression. In my experience, I have noticed that this section is almost always at the back of the store, rarely ever promoted up front (except, again, during Buwan ng Wika). Interestingly, I have also noticed that Filipino writers published by foreign publishing houses are shelved alongside foreign publications.

INVALIDATING INDIGENOUS SPIRITUALITY

Our thoughts and worldviews are often marginalized in our own spaces: Foreign thought is prioritized as more modern or advanced. I submitted an article to a journal a few years ago, discussing local beliefs about the spirits of nature. The editor kindly wrote back to me, requesting that I replace my use of the word *superstition* with *folk belief*. I had never considered this before, but I realized it was an example of my own sense of cultural inferiority. *Superstition* implies falsehood and compulsion—yet our beliefs are solidly grounded in an ancient worldview. They are not impractical, maladaptive habits; they carry earnest intentions aligned with deep cultural realities. I had unwittingly invalidated myself.

Many local scholars have also referred to folk beliefs as "pagan," distinct from urbanized Christianity, and local religious leaders have been clear about the supposed spiritual importance of letting go of folk beliefs. The exorcist Jose Francisco Syquia has warned many times that any attention or reverence given to local beliefs surrounding spirits, mystical items, and elementals can open the door to spiritual harassment and possession—in *Exorcism: Encounters with the Paranormal and the Occult,* Syquia indicates the clear danger of working with folk healers or even owning indigenous amulets. This "cult of spirits," he said, is merely idolatry.[4] Other sources of spiritual oppression, he said, can come from heavy metal music (which supposedly carries hypnotic subliminal messaging in favor of Satan), horoscopes, spirit questing (or paranormal investigation), and Transcendental Meditation.[5] He also advised that the deliverance ministry must assess whether any drug use or homosexual acts have occurred in the client's place, or whether antique items such as mirrors and paintings, which may harbor spirits, were recently added.[6]

I find Syquia's approach to be quite militant, which does makes sense within their worldview: Of course, if these spirits are real, they present a real danger. Everything he said is aligned with folkloric beliefs surrounding the supposed effects of angering an elemental (especially by bumping into them or cutting down a tree that may have been their home). What Syquia is encouraging, I think, is a clarity and firmness in one's religious beliefs, in contrast to the negotiations that local practitioners often do with whatever spiritual entity is present. In folk practice, it does not matter which spirit you are interacting with as long as you are on good terms. Syquia's point seems to be that you should be loyal to your spiritual patron, and in this way, they will protect you. It is easy to consider Syquia's approach to be a form of demonization, but in fact, he acknowledges and affirms the reality of indigenous spirits, and his gruesome and frightening anecdotes show his continued warfare against them. In other words, he does not set them aside as merely superstition, but rather as real hazards to one's well-being. If anything, I see Syquia's work as a kind of spiritual stubbornness, similar to the way a military general would be as they choose to willingly enter a battlefield of terror and bloodshed. Folk healers also recognize the dangers of illness, madness, and death associated with our interactions with spirits, but they also recognize the charisma associated with them.

In any case, as someone fascinated with the psychology of spirituality, I see folk beliefs as a great way to understand the cultural worldview. We see this in our paranormal anecdotes, forms of healing, and devotions to saints (which are, after all, modern-day anito, or ancestor spirits). It is not uncommon, to me at least, to hear someone I know interact with some kind of psychospiritual mystery—an entity or force, dream visitation, premonition, or miracle. My task, as a student of culture and human psychology, is to understand these from their point of view, and eventually to learn the appropriate methods of dealing with the irrational wonder of an unpredictable but meaningful life.

INVALIDATING FOOD, MUSIC, AND GAMES

Invalidation can manifest in so many other ways, especially with regard to the expressions of our culture. Filipino cuisine is a melting pot of influences and a manifestation of adaptation. Even though they may have been inspired by foreign dishes, all of our dishes are uniquely ours, not only in the ingredients used, but also in the way they are prepared. The combination of *kanin* (rice) and *ulam* (viand) can be considered part of our indigenous pattern of eating.[7] A hamburger is not like this, nor is sushi. We have so many amazing dishes, beyond the Filipinized ones—we know that there are differences in Pampango and Bicolano cuisine, and many more across various ethnolinguistic groups. I have always been proud of my home province's chicken *inasal*, a grilled chicken marinated in a fragrant, sweet, and salty sauce.* Across the country, there are slight variations in the preparation of certain types of *inihaw* (grilled meat), and in every house there are slight variations in your *tita's* (aunt's) adobo. Some add pineapple; others include eggs. I greatly enjoy videos of foreigners trying Filipino food for the first time, especially our take on fast food, but there is so much more than the usual selection of adobo, *balut*, and *halo-halo*.

In the field of music, the radio often plays original Pilipino music, or OPM—but how much of it is really Filipino? In the 1960s, we crooned like the jazz singers; in the 1970s and 1980s, we applied falsettos to our disco-infused music. In my youth, OPM was mostly Pinoy rock, which has very clear foreign influences. Today, our hip-hop seems to borrow heavily from whatever is popular in the United States. We are also seeing the rise of P-pop groups, obviously patterned after popular Korean groups. All this feels like we are appreciative of all genres, still, if anyone would immerse themselves in OPM, they would recognize distinctly Filipino attitudes and concerns—but expressed through foreign styles. One can hope for the eventual popularity of indigenous music, beyond token use during Buwan ng Wika. We do not have to stick to dated styles, but maybe we can still find inspiration in them and bring more of them into public consciousness. The issue is that if we focus too much on simply copying foreign styles, our music would just be local imitations—only good if they sound like what they are meant to emulate.

This extends to musicals too. In my experience, it feels somewhat out of touch for us to keep performing the culture-bound struggles of foreigners, wearing scarves and coats, and singing with a strange transpacific accent. For example, plays such as *Rent* and *In the Heights* are great representations for marginalized groups in specific contexts, and if we

---

* I was born in Negros Island.

are to find solidarity with communities around the world, there is nothing wrong with performing them here too. When I watched *Hamilton*, performed live in one of the massive local theaters, I found the production grand and the cast extremely talented. I even found the struggle for independence aligned with our own historical struggles. But most of these plays are all too American: That is not to say that they are bad, only that watching them feels so distinctly like a performance, and never like real life. Year after year it is the same foreign productions, and as much as I enjoy participating in these events, I do hope for more locally made productions that express our own joys and sorrows, that play with the musicality of our language. I watched one great play, *Pingkian: Isang Musikal*, based on the life and writings of an important historical figure rarely spoken about, Emilio Jacinto, a general in his early twenties who wrote many important subversive documents during the revolution against the Spanish colonizers. But the play itself, featuring an ambitious young man too smart for his own good, seems to follow in *Hamilton*'s footsteps: It is, like the American play, a rap musical. It could be that *Hamilton* opened some important creative doors for all other creatives, but that it should be a standard of quality and innovation only affirms having Western musicals be the center of theater culture. In any case, after watching it, I spent an entire month playing its soundtrack on repeat. It would be great if we could draw more from our experiences to inform richer and more enriching narratives. I am, of course, aware of the economic difficulties of the Philippine art scene, but I am also aware that there are many energetic artists who are very willing and very ready to create dangerously—if only we could be more courageous in supporting them.

We also pay so little attention to our indigenous games. As Enriquez pointed out, all that it takes for *laro* (games) to be formalized into *palaro* (sports) is a set of standardized rules.[8] But we see these games merely as childish interests—though I rarely see children play *tumbang preso, patintero,* or *langit-lupa* out in the streets anymore. The afternoons used to be loud with the laughter of children. Now, silence. It is also worth noting that we continue to succeed in many sports internationally—boxing, weightlifting, gymnastics, and others—and I hope that we could give the same consistent moral and financial support to those fields as we do with a sport like basketball, which was introduced to us by the Americans. It is interesting to see how we have adapted to it: Basketball is the game of friends, and it is also the way we socially assess the virility of a college or university. When I was studying in San Beda high school, the administration invested in our school spirit. But although our athletes played in other sports, we almost always just watched basketball. I never fully understood the rules of the game, but I knew enough to shout expletives at whoever our rival was. I am not sure whether it was school spirit, but it was some collective hysteria. Entering into Ateneo de Manila University, I was aware of its decades-long rivalry with De La Salle University—blue versus green, eagle versus archer. When my grand-uncle, a La Salle graduate, asked me where I was going to study for college, I said "Ateneo," and he said, in a low, teasing voice, "Stupid."

It is funny to me how playful school rivalries can be, and in some cases, how violent. Fights would erupt in arenas; players would be threatened; interschool romances would be forbidden. For many people, the potential of their undergraduate experience is actualized if their basketball team wins a championship during their time there. I was never that much into it back then, but, like I said, whenever I did get to watch the games and participate in the celebratory bonfires, it was always so exciting. Basketball is so ubiquitous in our everyday life that a *barangay* (the smallest administrative unit) would feel incomplete without a basketball court.

Destruction

Much has already been said about the outright destruction of our material culture by outside forces. Villages were burned by invaders and religious relics were destroyed. Until today, the echoes of war can still be heard in historical sites. Ghosts of the past haunt us: We still hear the

marching of bygone armies and the wails of abused women. We mourn
the loss of the past through its tangible memories, but on a more subtle
level, culture is also destroyed when it is desecrated or abandoned. It is
destroyed when sacred lands are turned into commercial areas, displac-
ing Indigenous communities. The Philippines is not a safe country for
Indigenous defenders and environmentalists, who experience harassment and human rights abuses. Unfortunately, not much is heard about
them, but they have been strong protectors of the land for decades, promoting a folk system of the respectful use of natural energy.[9]

The construction of the Kaliwa Dam, which would cut through the
Sierra Madre mountain range, was proposed to give Manila more access
to more water. Rather than rehabilitate existing sheds or embrace more
sustainable technology, the government approved foreign funding to
construct it, adversely affecting at least ten thousand members of the
Indigenous group known as the Dumagat-Remontado, and placing the
area's biodiversity at risk.[10] The Sierra Madre mountain range has a high
concentration of natural wealth and biodiversity; it has within it sixty-
eight protected areas and many native and threatened species.[11] It has
also been our protection against intense typhoons; in the old legend, she
is a mother who laid down her life for her children in the lowlands to
protect them from the evil king of storms.

Indigenous knowledge and environmentalism go hand in hand, and
folk worldviews and practices can inform future policies toward ethical
eco-friendly technology and human-oriented governance. Meanwhile,
profit-driven and exploitative industrialization has given us modern
comfort, massive wealth inequality, and the ongoing climate crisis. We
are seeing sweltering summers, worsening storms, higher floods, lost
islands, poisoned water, toxic air, and mass extinction of flora and fauna.
So, if we do not ground ourselves and innovate through nondominat-
ing methods in the near future, perhaps the comfort we experience with
industrialization will be short-lived. Hoarded wealth means nothing in
a burning world. Maybe this is the fate of humanity, but faced with our

impending apocalypse, maybe we can stop fooling ourselves into thinking that the world was created specifically for us, rather than us emerging from her womb. After all, as many before me have already pointed out, we are not killing the planet; we are only making it uninhabitable for us. The earth will live on—indeed our self-preservation aligns with the timeless wisdom of our ancestors, who lived with the spirits of nature and followed the world's rhythms.

DESTROYING INTUITIVE SYSTEMS

The ethics of colonialism, which values domination and control, manifests itself beyond the invasion of a foreign power. Philippine history is a history of political negotiations and bloody revolutions. Way back to our trading ancestors, we welcomed alliances with other cultures. But we never did well with forced subjugation, and since the victor writes the history books, the people's resistance and resilience are rarely, if ever, acknowledged. There were revolts across the archipelago when the Spanish came, and it took years for the United States to pacify the native revolutionaries. These histories are not always taught. I recall only when I was taking my undergraduate degree that I learned about these events. In elementary school, we were taught that Ferdinand Magellan "discovered" the Philippines in 1521 and that the United States came to liberate us from the Japanese during World War II. General Douglas McArthur's famous line, "I shall return," has been etched in my childhood psyche. I find it incredibly fascinating how the United States has managed its public image in the Philippine education system to the point that we welcomed the return of a foreign power that has economically and intellectually dominated us for years. I have heard some Filipino people say that it would have been great to be an American state, and, amid our current conflict with China, some people say that we cannot defend ourselves and that we definitely need the help of the United States. Many of our military materials are obsolete hand-me-downs from the United States. I am pointing this out simply to show the effects of cultural inferiority—we feel we cannot stand on our own feet, and we cannot see each other's strengths. Hierarchical thinking is a major influence here: We have gotten so used to being at the bottom that we have difficulty imagining what it would be like to be independent. On paper, we are supposedly independent, a recognized sovereign nation, and a free people. There is a genuine opportunity here to encourage local industries and bring indigenous wisdom to the world. Yet, for the most part, we are, intellectually, culturally, and spiritually tied to outsiders' standards. The effects of this are more violent than invalidation—we destroy the potential for the development of indigenous systems. Not only do we tend to invalidate indigenous wisdom per se, but we might also ignore the intuitive ways through which our physical environments could be maximized. Life becomes inconvenient for the everyday Filipino, and this unintuitive, foreign, imposed system affects almost every aspect of their life.

Something as simple as our school system's academic calendar, for example, was moved later in the year to match the "international" calendar, even though different countries have their own standards. Supposedly, this was done with the intention of global competitiveness. When I was in school, the summer break was April and May, the hottest months. The school year would start in June, have a Christmas break in December, and end in March. For all those years, it made sense. In 2015, the start was moved to August, and many children have had to suffer the intense heat of dilapidated classrooms during the summer months. Many school days were suspended because of this. One can say, however, that the new calendar is better since June and July are well-known to be part of the typhoon season.[12] Even then, graduation ceremonies are likely to be canceled or moved due to the rainy weather, and, especially in areas near stagnant water, dengue cases may rise. Nevertheless, the intense heat suffered in 2024 forced the government to quickly revert to the old schedule.[13] This is an interesting modern case of how we strive to be "globalized," even though we have other issues to consider: climate resilience, appropriate facilities, and better teacher compensation.

Commodification

In a global system where value is measured by profitability, and luxury is measured by scarcity, it is easy to sympathize with those who would sell their dignity to survive, especially if they have nothing material to give. This is the more pressing issue. We have a saying, *"Ang taong gipit, kahit sa patalim ay kakapit"* (Desperate people will cling on to anything, even a blade). This can imply criminal desperation, or holding onto what hurts us, thinking that it is the only thing we have. The Philippines is rich in biodiversity and people—yet we have been ransacked by invaders and exploited by our corrupt fellows. Sadly, we have internalized many of these exploitative ideas, and so we might unconsciously continue to perpetuate a system that continues to exploit us.

COMMODIFYING RESOURCES

I have noticed that we seem to be obsessed with being "world-class." Our fashion and media are expected to match international standards—even though "international" usually refers to the current trends in the United States or to a vague assumption of what "European" might look like. This extends to our tourist destinations, which are often compared to places outside the Philippines—our mountains are said to be like those in Switzerland or New Zealand, our beaches are like those in Bali or the Maldives, and our heritage towns are like Paris or Madrid. We have focused on making the Philippines recognizable enough for outsiders to feel comfortable visiting. But these sites are beautiful on their own. Just as Filipinos would visit other countries to experience their culture and environment, it should be that tourists visit the Philippines not because they want a cheaper, more hospitable version of foreign places, but, ideally, because they also want to experience our culture. That would, however, require that we know ourselves enough to embody our culture and be at home with our environment.

My hometown, Silay, is often called the "Paris of Negros" because of its heritage homes. Why not just *Silay*? It is beautiful on its own; why should we need to compare it anywhere else? Interestingly, *Paris* is not even used here in the sense of how it actually is, but rather in the metaphorical sense, of what people imagine Paris is like: filled with romance and art. The Eiffel Tower has no equivalent in Silay—how, then, can it be Paris-like? If we accept that *Paris* is used as a metaphor, then we have to critically assess the implication of its use: that Silay is merely a local imitation of a European city that does not have its own culture. But Silay is beautiful as it is, visually and historically. The San Diego Pro-Cathedral is a magnificent sight; at night its cross glows an ethereal neon blue. Statues of saints surround it, and within its domed structure, there are murals of biblical scenes. The altar is a towering wooden cabinet of saints and deities. The city center is organized like an old Spanish town, where the church, school, and city hall surround a plaza. On special occasions, the plaza is filled with smoke from the chicken *inasal* being cooked. During my recent visit, there was a line of tents, all selling grilled chicken and fish. There was also a beautiful procession attended by many of the locals.

Around the plaza are the houses of the old landed families that have been turned into museums for public viewing. Tour guides betray the family secrets of these old Ilustrados, whispering the memories of madness and forlorn lovers. Well-preserved paintings and furniture adorn these houses. Silay's history is romance, industry, and revolution. Subversives plotted the downfall of the Spanish colonial government in a drugstore along what is now Cinco de Noviembre Street, named after the day on which the local colonial power was ousted. Today, November 5 is Negros Day. Also, along Cinco de Noviembre is Balay Negrense, the ancestral house of the Gaston family, whose French patriarch, Yves Leopold Germain Gaston, introduced innovations to the local sugar industry. Perhaps this is where comparisons with Paris might make a little sense, but beyond this, barely anything can be said. It is all Silaynon.

The Philippines has a wealth of beautiful natural sites. The chilly islands of Batanes boasts gorgeous mountains and cliffs overlooking the vast ocean. I remember sitting on a cliffside in 2019, with no objection to either past or future, fully present. The beaches of Boracay, La Union, Zambales, El Nido, and Siargao are popular destinations for families, couples, solo travelers, and groups of friends. There is no need to compare them to any other place. In my experience, the nightlife is lively in many of these places; sit on mats and share conversations as the blazing sun sets on the horizon. There is nowhere else to be. You can also brave the narrow, steep, winding roads that lead to the northern mountains, where Indigenous communities still practice their ancient traditions. I visited the tattoo artists *(mambabatok)* in Kalinga and tried their local coffee, which was the strongest I have ever tasted. I did not go there to get a tattoo; I only wanted to meet the cultural icon Apo Whang-Od. Going back to Manila is a cultural experience in and of itself. I walked around the walled city of Intramuros. The stone churches, old cafés, and cobblestone streets can transport you to a pocket universe. I used to teach in a school within Intramuros, and I would often walk around. In Binondo, we would also find one of the world's oldest Chinatowns. Many people go there to participate in food crawls or purchase affordable jewelry. Once, many years ago, I joined an experimental walking tour of Manila that focused on abandoned buildings. So much architectural memory is lost to time. Manila is a pot of memories, cooked forever, stirred eternally.

COMMODIFYING PRECOLONIAL AESTHETICS

Perhaps in our younger days, we were much more open to dreaming about the future: It seemed like adults knew everything, and the world is filled with so much wonder that we are yet to experience. As children, we get so excited about what we do not know. Our youthful dreams may have been ridiculous, but they were almost always magnificent. The child sees the world and only begins to form an idea of it, and without knowing too much, they understand that everything is somehow connected. They will have to fill in the gaps, then, never mind the practical mathematics of how everyday things work. As we grow older, we confuse knowledge with disillusion; we think just because we know how the trick is done it is no longer effective. We eventually run out of tricks to marvel at, and the world becomes more and more real. Behind the mysterious closet door, which we may have once imagined to be a portal to the unknown, is just an inventory of cleaning materials. We were once asked what we would like to become, and many of us do not follow these dreams because reality gets to us first—many sudden and unplanned life events shift the trajectory of our original plans. Those of us who do get to follow our dreams eventually find out what these identities really entail. I am sure that it is very rare for someone to enjoy what they are doing every day. Those who do have found what the Japanese call their *ikigai,* or purpose.

Whatever the case, we also know there is pleasure in striving; it is exciting to dream and fight for liberation as much as (and, in many cases, more than) achieving it. We imagine it would be boring to do the same thing over and over. We create systems that keep us striving, longing, hoping, and fighting—and maybe, as a species, all these socioeconomic and political systems serve something much baser than we imagine. Order, structure, and protection from danger are all very important, but we have gamified it all with rewards and status. And there we have it: maybe a huge but ignored aspect of human systems is that it is a better alternative to boredom and waiting for death. But we have lost this charm. We are too deep in the game. Many of us—economists, politicians, academics— have made it their task to understand and play the game well and explain it to everyone else. Sadly, it is no longer amusing. There are just too many real consequences and too much undue influence on our chances of winning. In a bizarre twist of irony, the game we have collectively designed to stave off boredom has become existentially boring itself. The system intended to give us purpose by affirming that we can be whoever we want to become no longer works—or it only does for a select few.

Our experience of being here is only ever at *this* moment; there is, in truth, nothing else. Everything else is context, shaped by multiple simultaneously occurring moments. Sadly, the future no longer looks exciting; it no longer seems like a fertile land of potential, and most of us are hesitant to even plant our seeds. So, we look to the past. Because of material memory, we can reconstruct what happened, but we can never know for sure. Even something clearly written is shaped by the biases of their day— truthfully, this book you are holding now would probably not even pass the censor at any point in colonial history. It would have been burned, and I would have been arrested. Maybe I am just being dramatic, but this is an illustration of history from what I know about it, though I cannot confirm that it would have happened the way I described it here. Nevertheless, we like projecting our issues to the past: if we do not see any of our current problems being solved in the future, then maybe there are solutions in the old books or carvings, in the old traditions that have survived disastrous weather and destructive invaders. We think of time as linear when we do not interact with it linearly at all: Our schedules and appointments are scattered in time, triggered memories from long ago can be experienced today as though they are currently happening, and any history book will only ever tell one thread of memory. "World" histories conveniently leave out everything else in order to follow historical highlights—and what arrogance it is to claim to be the arbiter of what is historically "important." Most of world history is the political history of the ruling class; the poor and subjugated masses are often relegated to movements that overthrow the ruling class—and so, again, we see who was truly important.

Many human experiences and earthly wonders have been lost to time, and it is tempting for anyone in the social sciences to imagine more interesting interpretations of what could have happened in the past. But they have to work within what has been uncovered, through archaeology or careful ethnography. In these thousands of years maybe all thoughts have already been thought and all feelings already felt, and if we were humans hundreds of thousands of years ago, the range of our joys and sorrows today may have been the same back then, only in different contexts. But we cannot be stopped from dreaming. That is what we humans do: We are constantly striving and longing and hoping and fighting. We already have many different and important reasons, so maybe we can also accept one more fundamental reason: that it is all very, very fun.

However, more often than not, we tend to construct fictional stories and claim that they are true. If we had not been colonized, we would have had a very different fashion sense, or we would still be writing in the ancient scripts, or we would be a Muslim or Buddhist or Hindu country. These stories may be true, but, nonetheless, they are imagined possibilities and fantasies of what did not happen. Like the dreaming of a child, we are filling the gaps and reconstructing the world based on how we should hope for it to look. We might go back to writing in *baybayin,* one of the many ancient scripts in the Philippines, but we are only translating modern thought into coded language. The old writings were poems and social negotiations. Today, baybayin is used as the logo of new cafés or inappropriately applied to various signage. It would be wonderful if we could relearn how to use our indigenous scripts meaningfully, but for now, we know that it is just an aesthetic preference, used commercially in the same way that East Asian scripts have been endlessly fetishized in non-Asian films and tattooed onto oblivious tourists' bodies.

In the same vein, we appropriate the designs of existing Indigenous communities, accepting the imagination that, maybe, because they have retained their unique designs, their clothes are what used to be worn in the past. This may be true, but its historical truthfulness is secondary in importance to its symbolic truthfulness, in that it "feels" authentic. Thus, without really knowing much about the lore of woven patterns and indigenous tattoo designs, we wear these aesthetics proudly—this is more of an affirmation of personal identity than a way to represent the culture. These patterns are produced mechanically and sold decontextualized. The patterns may be accurate, but the soul has gone. The indigenous designs found in large malls—on jackets, vests, kimonos, and shirts—are corpses. Were these modern clothes made by weavers and dreamers? Do the proceeds of this sale support them? Maybe we are just drawn to the old patterns. There is nothing wrong with that. But do we know what we are wearing? And if we do not care, then we have become so lost to the meaning-making of our own heritage.

We also speak of our ancestors as though they were a homogenous group of wise elders. Because our modern society does not give us the purpose we crave, we look fondly to a time when we assume that people knew what they were supposed to do and to be, a more spiritual time. *Indigenous wisdom* becomes interchangeable with *ancestral wisdom*. The difference is that the latter is passed on by wise sages whose names have been forgotten, whereas the former grows from wherever we are. In other words, what is ancestral is what has been handed down; what is indigenous is what emerges from context, here and now. The work being done in the social sciences is very important, and all professionals and practitioners deserve to be well-compensated for their intellectual and spiritual labor so that they can continue to pursue important cultural endeavors. There are, however, many ways through which indigenous wisdom, particularly those related to folk spirituality, are commodified for the aesthetic or "vibe" and not necessarily for its cultural importance. Those borrowing from ancient traditions ought to respect history and culture and, if possible, the involvement of its living practitioners. But there are too many workshops, retreats, and well-being services claiming to be properly indigenous, yet they are only partially so—or are only indigenous in appearance. The wisdom is found not in the aesthetic but in what the aesthetic represents. As Grace Nono points out, the practices of the Philippine orator-mystic, known primarily as *babaylan,* have been marginalized; first by colonizers, now by us.[14] While it is historically true that they have been suppressed by the colonizers, they have in fact persisted in various ways—the urban babaylan is the folk practitioner at the corner of your street who knows the secret wisdom of plants and the hidden names of God. The babaylan tradition still does exist as an indigenous system; they still sing in the mountains and forests. Yet it is more convenient for the workshop organizer to appropriate indigenous customs when they imagine the source of these customs to be long gone. There is a romance in unearthing and recovering what was once lost, and if we are seeking to unearth that which lies dormant within us earnestly, we might just pay handsomely for this experience.

Unfortunately, in our current system of profit and value, abstract concepts are difficult to sell; aesthetics are more tangible and are much more easily appraised. The funny thing is that all this wisdom was never for sale anyway, and it is accessible to anyone who begins their journey to embody the mythic potential of their inner self.

Power and Mythology

Historically, the local elite, or burgis, continued to find ways to work with the colonizers toward fair and mutually beneficial conditions. This benefited them only, leaving the masses to adapt their indigenous customs to appease them. The burgis have historically prioritized themselves, operating on a kaniya-kaniya mindset to make the most out of difficult situations. Whenever it was beneficial to them, the burgis allied themselves with the people to promote the goals of the nation, but the old landed families have always been in power. In this way, the hierarchical mindset of the old colonizers has continued to persist, wherein the archipelago's wealth belongs to everyone but the natives.

When Ferdinand Marcos Sr. was elected as president in 1965, he deftly applied nationalistic mythology to solidify his power. His wife, Imelda, was a patron of the arts, and she encouraged extravagant architectural projects to promote Philippine culture. She was well-known for her love of shoes, and today, the Shoe Museum in Marikina City features her special collection and a massive, elegant portrait of the madame. The Marcoses used our ancient creation myths to affirm their status as the parents of the nation: They presented themselves as Malakas (strong) and Maganda (beautiful), the first man and woman to emerge from the primordial bamboo.[15] Positioning themselves as archetypal parents, they tapped into the powerful psychological tendency for children to "honor your mother and father." This was part of their artful strategy, which informed the political propaganda of the time. Time and again, leaders in the government, religious cults, or even in everyday organizations are seen as parents—a good leader is stern but caring, compassionate but orderly. I have worked in organizations where female leaders were called "Mama" or "Tita." Former president Rodrigo Duterte was, during his administration, affectionately called "Tatay (Daddy) Digong," and anyone who would not follow his policies were considered *pasaway* (stubborn), like children who disobeyed the orders of their parents.

Recently, another story has been passed around on social media relating the Marcoses, involving a so-called Maharlika kingdom, whose supposed ruler, the Tallano family, allegedly provided for the great wealth of the Marcoses in the form of gold bullion. Of course, there is no recorded archaeological proof of this, at all.[16] But this seemed to be helpful in the grand scheme of the Marcoses' return to power—Ferdinand "Bongbong" Marcos Jr. was elected the seventeenth president of the Philippines in 2022.

The era of Marcos Sr. was a troublesome time. His economic policies gave foreign investors full access to local resources, making simple goods such as bananas too expensive for ordinary Filipinos. Marcos Sr's family and friends were also well taken care of: His cronies controlled most of the vital local industries. Faced with dire poverty, many Filipinos were forced to move abroad to find better prospects. Many Filipinos were starting to get restless, and protests began to challenge the Marcos Sr. regime. On September 23, 1972, Marcos Sr. announced that the country would be placed under martial law, allegedly to suppress subversion. Interestingly, as historians Mariel N. Francisco and Fe Maria C. Arriola pointed out, his pacification techniques were very similar to those used by the Americans.[17] The Sedition Law of 1901 made it punishable to speak about independence—during martial law, there was the Anti-Subversion Act, where even rumormongering was criminalized. The Reconcentration Act of 1903 imposed curfews, where violators were shot on sight—similarly, the martial law era was known for "salvaging," which involved military torture and abuse of captured civilians. The Flag Law Act of 1907 suppressed national sentiment by prohibiting any display of the Philippine flag—the song "Bayan Ko" (My Country), originally written by the revolutionary José Alejandrino during the Philippine-American War, was often sung by anti-Marcos protestors, and it was eventually banned.

In February 1986, fed up with electoral cheating and economic difficulties, and spurred on by the assassination of the opposition leader Benigno "Ninoy" Aquino Jr., the people—students, church leaders, professionals, and even the burgis—came together and marched along Epifanio de los Santos Avenue (known as EDSA). This show of solidarity among hundreds of thousands of Filipinos is now known as the People Power Revolution, a peaceful revolution that forced the Marcoses to flee, placing in power the widowed wife of Ninoy, Maria Corazon "Cory" Aquino. It is worth noting that the Aquinos are also burgis, in that they come from the wealthy landed aristocracy. Nevertheless, in history, we see that the only thing that can defeat myth-making is alternative myth-making. Cory was seen as the archetypal mother: Mary, the suffering mother of God.[18] One lesson we can take away from this is that it is vital that we know our own psychology and be at home with our own folklore because if we do not, we risk being manipulated by those who do. Furthermore, the mindset of the colonizer is not something so foreign to us; it is a human thing, and as such, so long as societal power is hierarchical, cultural dominance can happen.

We have seen how cultural domination can be both subtle and pervasive, affecting us without our conscious knowledge. We affirm these ideas because we are always exposed to them, believing them to be just how things are. But noticing how inconvenient things are should allow us to take a step back enough to reassess what does work for us. We can begin to notice how we tend to degrade the way we look, speak, sing, write, dance, play games, and so on. Why is it that many things that come from us feel cringey or juvenile? If we cannot simply invalidate our own intuitive ways of being, we tend to destroy what makes us who we are—knowledge systems emerging from generational interaction with environments and communities are wiped out. And if we cannot invalidate or destroy, we make do with what we have: We sell it as an aesthetic removed from actual lifestyle. We say they are like better foreign things, but cheaper. Things and places are commodified, taken apart and sold piece by piece. Being aware of how internalized cultural inferiority can lead to invalidation, destruction, and commodification, we can now challenge the process of cultural domination through *recognition, preservation, dialogue,* and *collaboration.*

CHAPTER SIX

-

Authenticity

Culture is internalized and embodied by individuals; individuals, in turn, shape culture as they participate in its continued transformation. Cultural memory is the memory of people. As individuals, we may not have been alive during moments of Filipino history such as the conquest of the Spaniards (1565–1898), the "benevolent assimilation" of the United States (1898–1946), the occupation of the Japanese (1942–1945), or the Marcos Sr. dictatorship, especially the martial law period starting in 1972 until the People Power Revolution of 1986, just as many people born today will not have been alive during the street killings of suspected drug dealers during the Duterte presidency, known as the War on Drugs (2016–2022). Life will be very different for the coming generations. Still, they will carry the echoes of history, not only in the media they consume, created by our generation and the generations before us, but through cultural adaptation that was necessary for our survival in trying times. Our cultural evolution is banana ketchup, developed due to a lack of tomatoes; it is jeepneys, modified from military vehicles from the American era; it is the Sinulog festival, which is the persistence of ancient worship despite centuries of Christianization. Nick Joaquin commented that if we removed adobo and *pandesal* from our everyday life, pointing out that these are Western imports, the every-day Filipino might find that ridiculous because these things are inseparable parts of who we are, like our bones, our skin, our voice.[1]

Colonization is the dual process of intruding *(panghihimasok)* and assimilating *(pananakop)*. Decolonization is the removal of mindsets and structures imposed by outsiders, which tend to be either useless or misaligned with what is intuitive to locals. Because our colonizers have been Westerners, we have conflated decolonization with the absolute removal of everything Western. This essentialism relies on stereotypes and denies the agency of our ancestors as they resisted, confronted, and assimilated foreign ways. In other words, we might remove everything considered to be "Western" regardless of whether or not they are useful, thereby isolating our culture from everything else, creating walls between vague yet militaristic definitions of Filipino and non-Filipino.

Romanticizing the Exotic

Our dissatisfaction with the effects of commodified globalization has inspired us to look for the "purely" indigenous, which is, in fact, a form of romanticizing the exotic—we have become so alienated by the bland conveniences and meaningless production of modern life that we seek to reconnect with "ancestral wisdom." But they were just as human as we are today, only without vaccines, forty-hour work weeks, online shopping, credit cards, airplanes, social media doomscrolling, and so on. (There are things for every age, wherever you go in time; we will still be human—ambitious, hungry, gullible, and wise.)

It is easy to project our imagined solutions for the present onto the past, because the past is a totally different culture, and, more importantly, because the past is dead. It is much easier to define that which no longer transforms. You can hold it, manipulate it, use it for your own agenda, and the past will not complain. It is much more difficult to confront the ever-changing present, with its constantly shifting realities. So, it makes absolute sense, given our current predicament, to want to "return to the precolonial" and dream of what we could have been if we were not colonized. But we must also recognize that this is, first and foremost, a reaction to modern realities, an idealization of what we could have today if things were just more convenient for everyone. The past holds much wisdom, and its application will be toward the future. Let us look, with clear eyes, at how we have truly transformed, rather than blindly succumb to false nostalgia.

Today, we see that, despite our blood-soaked revolutionary history, Philippine culture has absorbed and localized many symbolic and technological imports, partly out of imposition, mostly out of practicality. If you pay close attention, you will see that the Filipinized expression of foreign things does not necessarily conform to their "traditional" counterpart. For example, Philippine Christianity has been adapted to express indigenous spirituality. Observe the devotional practices *(panata)* for the saints, such as Hesus Nazareno, Santo Niño, and for regional varieties of Our Lady—they are expressions of what was once known as *pag-anito*, the shamanic negotiation between man and divine. Even the deification of the cultural hero Jose Rizal among the Rizalistas shows us the similar process undergone by the epic heroes—for as Jesus Christ died to ensure our spiritual liberation from sin, it is believed that Rizal died for the Philippine freedom.[2] Many things with foreign origins—in language, cuisine, custom, and so on—have become so "Filipinized" that we no longer feel that they are apart from our own "authentic" identity. That is because culture is not merely archaeological; it is something that is lived and shaped by physical and social environments.

We know, of course, that the trauma of colonization has convinced us of our own inferiority. This is an attitude we call "colonial mentality," but I prefer A. A. Phillips's term *cultural cringe*.[3] We see this in the way we tend to belittle anything "made in the Philippines," even if (and perhaps especially if) they have a hint of the foreign. Thinking about it, in the history of the world, there is barely anything so original to one culture to claim that it belongs to that culture and that culture alone—once again, as Joaquin pointed out, other cultures retell their histories by describing the influence of imported technology on their own progress; meanwhile, we retell our history almost with annoyance that we were bothered by outsiders.[4] We like to think that we were once "pure," and then we were forever tainted by colonization—it is the same rhetoric as the archaic and misogynistic myth of virginity. True to form, and taken to the extreme, we have always portrayed colonization as the rape of poor Luzviminda (a feminized portmanteau of Luzon, Visayas, and Mindanao). Albert Alejo pointed out that there are parallels between rape *(gahasa)* and colonization, in that both involve panghihimasok and pananakop.[5] Therefore, this visceral metaphor extends from the personal to the national, echoing the violence of exoticization and exploitation.

So, when we call to "go back" to the precolonial, where shall we go? How far back, and which specific era of the precolonial? Here, we are confronted with the actual problem: that our desire to find ancestral wisdom tends to be a selective regression into an arbitrary and archetypal precolonial era, with aesthetics loosely borrowed from old books and surviving Indigenous communities. The irony is that these old books were likely written by European explorers—thus, the image we have of the precolonial native is not even our own! It is, in truth, simply an aesthetic—that is, a surface-level—form of decolonization. The costume is ancient, but the wearer is modern, so we go back to the old proverb: *Ang unggoy, damitan mo man, unggoy pa rin.* (Dress a monkey up and it's still a monkey.) Aesthetic decolonization—which might look like a forced return to ancient scripts or wearing ethnic patterns and tattoos without knowing the meaning—is just a pretension, a costume, an appropriation of a culture that is not actually ours, what we call pagpapanggap.

Pagpapanggap can be a form of pananakop, in the sense that one's outward appearance does not really emerge from within. It takes ethnic objects only to display them, as certain museums today still do when they display the stolen artifacts from colonized people. A person can be very knowledgeable about cultural things—they may even speak the language fluently—but if their interiority operates in the terms and frameworks of a foreign worldview, their exterior is nevertheless fake. We must remember that this is how the *mananakop* (colonizer) enters insidiously: They import their values using local symbols and languages.

Becoming Culturally Authentic

I understand that the previous section may rub certain people the wrong way. It might be taken as an attack or as a form of gatekeeping. If it is taken as an attack, reflect on this feeling. Why is it offensive to be called out for one's shallow use of cultural aesthetics? If you do know the meaning of the symbols you wear, and you wear them proudly because you understand their relevance, why would you take offense to the previous section? Again, I did not say, "Do not use ethnic designs at all!" I said, "If you are going to use ethnic designs, particularly from a culture that you are not totally familiar with, it would be respectful to, at least, learn their meanings."

Early in my research, I shared my interpretations of certain tattoo designs from the north, taking inspiration from my readings on indigenous dream symbolism. At the time, I did not think anything I did was wrong. After all, these designs were shared heritage, and people seemed to resonate with my interpretations well. A tattoo artist messaged me privately to offer some corrections, pointing out that certain tattoo designs were not indigenous. One of the designs, for example, was a compass, and it did not even occur to me that compasses may have been imported technology. Being corrected was embarrassing, but I learned to be more respectful about the nuances of culture. Although I am Filipino, I do not share the particular culture of tattooed communities. Since then, I only talked about beliefs and customs I am truly immersed in, things I can confidently say I know. In other areas, I do not have to pretend; I will happily be a student.

If you were not born into a particular culture, you immerse yourself until you become one with the people of that culture, until you both speak and think like them, until you see yourself in them. Absorb music, art, literature. Dance in conversation with others. The most subtle block that will prevent you is the tendency to categorize and find equivalence—drop all "universal" assumptions you may have and enter with the full appreciation of an empty cup.

If you were born into the culture, identify the small ways you are betraying it—for this, go back to the previous chapter.

The process of decolonization is a return to authenticity. Authenticity is *pagpapakatotoo,* a word that refers to the act of embodying truth. It involves the alignment of loob (interior) and *labas* (exterior). For a long time, scholars within the Philippine social sciences have shown great interest in the concept of loob, because of how it appears in our language. Loob, by itself, simply refers to the "inside" of something. If we are curious about the contents of a box, we would ask, *"Ano ang nasa loob ng kahon?"* (What is inside the box?) But loob also appears in a variety of ways, expressing its multiple dimensions. *Vicassan's Pilipino-English Dictionary* defines *loob* as an interior, but also as will, disposition, courage, and manners.[6] In Rogelia Pe-Pua's unpacking of this concept, multiple linguistic and philosophical implications abound.[7] Reynaldo Ileto's interpretation of loob as an egalitarian interiority where all people are free draws from his analysis of the early Philippine revolution as a transformation of the inner self. Leonardo Mercado identified loob as the intellectual, emotional, and ethical part of sarili (self). Zeus Salazar and Albert Alejo envisioned loob as something that touches on and embodies collective realities while reaching out to others. Pe-Pua also discussed various implications of loob's linguistic attachments, which function as adjectives to describe one's loob. Loob can have intention *(kusa),* durability *(tibay),* and valor *(dakila).* It can be truthful *(tapat)* and at ease *(palagay).* It can also be renewed *(bago)* or it can return to its original state *(balik).* Loob also has various binary associations, such as strength *(lakas)* and weakness *(hina),* good *(buti)* and bad *(sama),* and open *(bukas)* and closed *(sarado).* I am only scratching the surface here; these words, and many more, imply a world of meaning, especially in how they are applied. A person suspicious of someone's intentions says that the other person might be *masamang loob* (a bad person masquerading as a good one), so they feel a sense of discomfort around them *(hindi mapalagay ang loob)*. That other person may hide a boiling rage *(nasa loob ang kulo)*. A person who is a wonderful companion can make one feel light, and so we might say, *"Magaan ang loob ko sa kaniya"* (I feel light around them). A beautiful interiority *(kagandahang-loob)* can be recognized through charitable actions *(kabutihang loob)*, but only when it is done willingly *(kusang loob)*, emerging from one's interiority *(bukal sa loob)* and shared with an open heart *(bukas loob)*. Although it is a Tagalog word, it is not just a Tagalog experience; there are parallels between the Bisaya *buot* and the Ilokano *nakem*.[8] The will of a person is *kalooban/kabubut-on/pakinakem*. One might also refer to the need to repay with gratitude as *utang na loob/ utang-buot/utang a naimbag a nakem*. Goodness can be described as *katapatang-loob/buotan/nanakem*. Here, we see that variety in language is an access point to a shared human reality, regardless of where we are.

The loob of a person, then, refers to the living inner world within an individual. From it comes the intuition of social dynamics and the understanding of symbols. One's loob, manifested in their personhood (katauhan), is expressed through the body (katawan). The expression of one's identity emerges from within *(mula sa loob)*: It is meant deeply and with love. The act of loving is called *pag-ibig*, and *ibig* refers to sincerity. The phrase *ibig sabihin* refers to something a person *really* wants to say *(saloobin)*, a truth from the deepest self *(kalooban)*. The friend is *kaibigan*: it is *ibig* (sincerity), with the prefix *ka* (connection, like the English *co-*) and the suffix *-an* (participative action, such as in chasing games, *habulan*, or hiding games, *tagu-taguan*). Having a friend implies, therefore, the shared act of sincerity. The act of friendship, *pakikipagkaibigan*, has the additional prefix *paki-*, which implies a request. (For example, *paki-usap* means "Please consider.") The act of friendship, then, is a request for deeper sincerity, a call for shared vulnerability, or *pakikipagpalagayang-loob*—that is, "Please *(paki-)* place *(lagay)* your interiority (loob), as I am also sharing

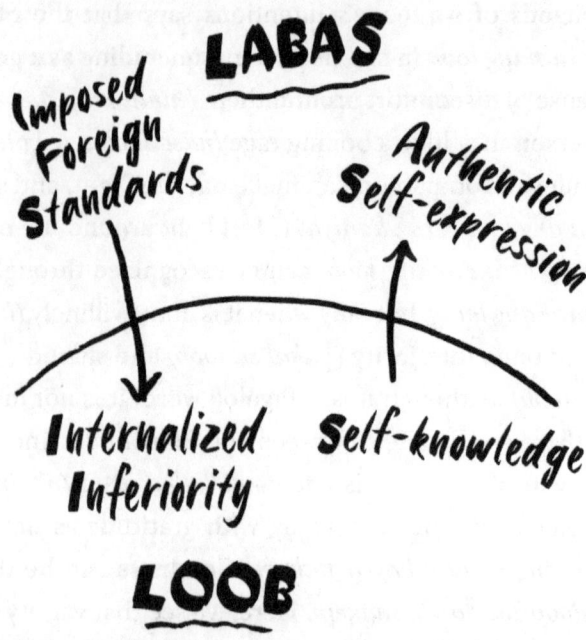

Figure 6.1. The relationship between *Loob* and *Labas* and
how this influences authentic self-expression

mine." The English translation, "rapport," is too shallow, too tenuous, too
fragile. No, true friendship is shared vulnerability, and it is here that we
find strength.

The individual loob can eventually be aligned with the divine will, or
loob ng Maykapal, and that is when real transformation occurs, which
we call *pagbabagong-loob* (inner change). The inner self or loob is only
whole *(buo ang loob)* when the individual makes a commitment—and this
commitment is eternal and unwavering. It is here that a person acts and
that a person becomes truly authentic.

Reclaiming Authenticity

The antidote to cultural domination is flourishing despite it. The first
response is of course resistance, but this can only go so far, as it will

always be operating with the standard of the oppressor. We defend ourselves to correct the claims of the oppressor. We promote ourselves in contrast to the oppressor—that is, we turn them into a hollow image and constantly talk about ourselves by comparing our traits with theirs. It will be layers upon layers of thin but angry rhetoric. Until we figure ourselves out, based on our own standards, the discussion will perpetually be us versus the rest of the world. We become more and more isolated when we should be more and more connected—with allies nearby and allies in the very heart of the oppressor's land. We must resist, but on our own terms, and flourish by nourishing each other. We do this through *recognition, preservation, dialogue,* and *collaboration.*

RECOGNITION

There is something to be said about the power and hypocrisy of Pinoy Pride, wherein Filipinos around the world are celebrated when they are recognized by the international community—even though they are barely recognized here. Since foreign standards are still the norm, we might only feel validated when we are witnessed by outsiders. Certain online content creators use this as a gimmick: The mere mention of anything remotely Filipino encourages engagement—something that is now known as Pinoy baiting. It is great to celebrate each other, but why do we only do so to meet the standards of others? So many talents—in the arts, sciences, sports, literature, and more—are severely underfunded. Many professionals would rather seek a better life abroad, thus leading to a brain drain. A child who shows some artistic inclinations might be confronted by a sarcastic parent saying, *"Ano ipapakain mo sa mga anak mo? Pintura?"* (What will you feed your children? Paint?) This line is quite common; it has become something of a meme. Of course, the parent has a right to worry. Life is not easy, and it is not easy to make a living in the arts. The most assured path, they say, is a finished education, because most employers only hire graduates. *"Tapusin mo lang pag-aaral mo, at bahala ka na sa buhay mo pagkatapos."* (Finish your studies first, and then do whatever you want.) Education becomes a parent's obligation, and a child's opportunity to succeed—but it is more like a lottery ticket because success is never assured. In the end, we rarely, if ever, nourish our children's passions. We have become a nation with many educated laborers, and cheap work for hire—a systemic issue that also has roots in the persistence of neocolonial structures. And because we cannot afford to live in our own country, we seek opportunities elsewhere. When children graduate abroad or move to another country for work, it becomes a source of pride for their parents. Who, then, is left here?

Recognition as a reclamation of authenticity involves acknowledging local talent and its nourishment toward sustainable nation-building. Instead of merely producing humans as products for the global market, we can encourage artistic and scientific innovation here. Another form of recognition is listening to recommendations from local researchers on how to improve societal systems instead of ignoring their suggestions. One lawmaker did this when they questioned a budget request for more agricultural research: "You are all too crazy about research. What the hell will you do with that research? I am a smart person, but I do not understand why you need to do that—the farmer would prefer more seeds and more machinery, not more research!"[9] I have paraphrased for impact, but the original comment became a sore point that echoed the dismal state of funding in the local sciences.

PRESERVATION

We know that so much has already been destroyed, so what matters more now is the preservation of culturally relevant materials and existing areas. I have already discussed the importance of preserving ecological biodiversity—just as important are things like books and historical architecture.

Unfortunately, many vital sources of ethnic knowledge are now out-of-print and difficult to find. We must make the most of existing technology to digitize old books, especially those written by local ethnographers on indigenous knowledge systems. If you do not know what you are looking

for, you will probably not find it. Even in my research, I am always surprised to find out that there have already been entire books written about
niche topics that fascinate me. For example, one of my primary interests is
the paranormal, especially how it manifests in Philippine culture through
folklore and strange everyday phenomena. In a psychology class I was
teaching, a student group presented on the Filipino paranormal, citing,
of all people, Virgilio Enriquez, who had written about the paranormal
in the Philippines years ago. At the time, I did not know this; the only
local scholar I knew who talked about the paranormal in a psychological context was Jaime Bulatao. Finding Bulatao's book was also a chance
encounter, as I picked it up in a bargain bin over a decade ago. Similarly,
finding Enriquez's monograph on the paranormal was pure luck. A local
psychology library had donated a massive pile of dusty old books. They
lay scattered on the floor of the building where I held classes. I had a feeling *(kutob)* that Enriquez's monograph was there, and I found multiple
copies. Only recently did I find out, through a different essay also written by Enriquez, that others had already been talking about the Filipino
paranormal before this monograph. I found a very fragile copy in one of
the old libraries. We must appreciate Enriquez and his peers' determination to produce indigenous academic research during a tumultuous time
(they flourished during the martial law era). Through an arduous search,
I found dated essays on psychic warfare, psycholinguistics, dream interpretation, and ethnopsychiatry. I would not be surprised to learn I am the
only one who has read these articles in decades. It is telling that I could
purchase many copies of indigenous academic books not through the
local publishers who originally sold them but through foreign sources.
These important books should be locally available, not just imported. We
produce, but we barely preserve. For Filipinos who might be interested in
these things, their entrance to this incredible field would likely be foreign
thinkers and foreign publications first.

Also, many old historical buildings are being demolished to make way
for gaudy commercial centers, or they are left to rot. When I was younger,

I participated in a walking tour of old Manila, and it was disheartening to see gorgeous buildings succumbing to their dilapidation. The stories of these structures were of rich community histories and glamorous gatherings—but now they stand as shadows of their former selves, unused and somewhat forgotten to anyone who is still alive to remember. When the Manila Central Post Office, built during the American colonial era, caught on fire in 2023, there was a renewed call to rehabilitate other historical sites.[10] Most of the well-preserved buildings are tourist attractions, so this is where ethical tourism can be a great ally for the preservation of material culture.

Documenting and archiving folk heritage are also very important. You can start with your own experience. Instead of looking for definitions elsewhere, define what culture means to *you,* and describe how you live it with the people you love. Tell us how cultures and preferences intersect. Collect the memories of your elders, their proverbs and riddles, their strange idioms that, once analyzed, carry mysterious cultural weight. See if you can consciously apply ancient wisdom to your modern experiences. See what intuitively works. By embodying culture, you become a culture-bearer.

DIALOGUE

I have discussed the importance of cultural, cross-indigenous dialogue in chapter 3. I reiterate its importance here. Dialogue can be a path toward greater authenticity in that it allows for the participation of nuanced perspectives. If *indigenous* refers to what naturally emerges from a culture, then *cross-indigenous* dialogue is when people talk about their own lived experiences at a table where everyone shares the same meal. To be clear, *indigenous* does not refer to one's country alone. When we talk about Filipino psychology, we are not referring to a Filipino national psychology, or psychology in the Philippines. Creating a generalization about all Filipinos based on broad and idealized strokes of cultural personality is a lazy way of thinking. More often than not, this way of thinking privileges urban and Westernized centers, which is not the experience of every Filipino. But also, when we talk about "indigenous," we are not only referring to Indigenous communities, in that their psychology is the "right" psychology of Filipinos. To even say that Indigenous communities are "more Filipino" is an ironic statement, being that *Filipino* becomes a foreign term unfairly applied to them. We risk spiraling farther and farther in these linguistic games of idealized realities because, in a world that needs assurance of truth in terms of defined, material fact, there is a need to exclude things. These othered things go nowhere.

Then, if Filipino psychology is the psychology of Filipinos, we are forced to define what *Filipino* is in terms of material fact—but what do we consider relevant information? We can concretely define Filipino-ness through government documents—but we know that, even within the archipelago, we often say that some people are more culturally aligned than others in some way. We also say that some people, even non-Filipinos, are somehow "more Filipino." So, we know that one's culture is not just whatever is written on paper. We can also concretely define Filipino-ness by one's birthplace or one's genetic heritage. But just because one was born in a certain place does not mean that they were also born with that culture, as if it were something inherent—if they are raised elsewhere, they might not speak the language or understand the cultural nuances of their place of birth but will most likely know the spirit of their lived places. One cannot lose a culture they did not know, but one can adapt and embody new and different cultures.

Although genetic heritage says a lot about a person, it also matters little if one is not exposed to particular things through which innate abilities and vulnerabilities might be triggered or enhanced. One's physical appearance carries certain privileges and disadvantages through which social resources can be accessed or blocked, regardless of who or what we are. Family or peer influence can keep a child rooted in a culture, no matter how far away it may feel, but as different cultures interact, people tend to assimilate into the dominant culture. One's participation in culture depends on whether one also participates in its continued transformation. All that being said, for indigenous psychology to be relevant at all, it must be intersectional. It must recognize differences within societies that generally share the same culture—however, this culture will be expressed in so many different ways. One's socioeconomic class influences what one has access to (education, media, and so on), which can also influence what culture they embody. We can talk about "Westernized" Filipinos in this way—Filipinos who, despite being born in the Philippines, and despite having lived here for their entire life, act as though they were of a different culture or nationality. Their language, references, and preferences are foreign.

So now we are going deeper and deeper into things, but only to make a point. In truth, these things are only scratching the surface. These things only look at culture as though it were something to be performed. That is why it is so important to recognize loob as an access point toward greater authenticity. One's interiority, which contains the internalized aspects of culture, is embodied and expressed naturally. Discourse toward greater authenticity is a discourse across different aspects of culture, not just across nations, but within societies, and more so within communities. Cross-indigenous dialogue is not just between cultures from different countries, such as Filipinos, Kenyans, and Canadians, although this is valuable too. It is also between different communities within a society, such as various Asian American communities, or across various Indigenous communities in the Philippines. We could say that a true Filipino psychology can be found in the participation of more Filipinos, here and abroad.* Cross-cultural studies have a clear source (an authority) through which other cultures are assessed and judged. Cross-indigenous dialogue is when a shared, nonhierarchical space provides people with the

---

* A good approximation to this was the metalinguistic analyses of Leonardo Mercado, who had written on the varieties and similarities among Tagalog, Bisaya, and Ilokano languages as an approach to indigenizing philosophy.

opportunity to come from their own contexts. We learn through dialogue; culture is preserved through dialogue.

COLLABORATION

For many indigenous psychologists, their work is advocacy. When we feel (pakikiramdam) with others, we internalize their struggle—or, put another way, we find that their struggles reflect our own. This is when our loob reaches outward. It can sense others *(abot-malay)* and feel with them *(abot-dama)*, and, when one is filled with conviction *(buo ang loob)*, one reaches out *(abot-kaya)*.[11] During the COVID-19 pandemic, various community pantries started popping up across the country as a response to delays in government assistance, especially for the marginalized. It started in Maginhawa Street by Ana Patricia Non, with the tenet *Magbigay ayon sa kakayahan, kumuha batay sa pangangailangan* (Give what you can, take only what you need).[12] This is a modern example of the old virtue of bayanihan, which is the collective act of carrying a house and moving it from one place to another. It has now come to mean cooperation, especially for one's kapwa. One becomes a hero (bayani) for each other.[†] We also see this in times of disaster, such as during typhoon season, when many homes are flooded and destroyed, and many people need evacuation and shelter. Helping each other gets much easier with a sense of shared identity. This is a realization that we are, fundamentally, the same, in that we share the same humanity.

But collaboration is not just a disaster response, it is also an active effort to make things more convenient—that is, more intuitive to the movements of the local spirit. We tend to fall into the trap of kaniya-kaniya, especially when we do not feel that we share the struggle. We have gotten used to *diskarte* (strategies), *kapit* (connections), and *lusot* (loopholes) as a way of life. We have been called "resilient" for our efforts,

---

† Note again the use of *-an* as a suffix, implying that the root word becomes something we collectively participate in.

yet I cannot help but think that a system working efficiently will not need separate strategies other than following the right process. If something works, we will not need to contact friends in the system, look for loopholes, or prepare our strategies. We would not need to be "resilient" all the time if we were cared for by the people we trusted with power. We would not have to rely on bayanihan, as beautiful as it is, if we could afford meals, clean water, clothes, and shelter. Why is it our responsibility to individually navigate the system in place? Does this not mean that the system is unintuitive?

The inconveniences we experience as everyday Filipinos, in terms of, for example, public transportation or required social procedures, especially in government offices, reflect larger social concerns. It is not only a matter of waking up earlier to catch the first jeepney ride or waiting hours before the offices open to be first in line. We must ask ourselves: Are the pathways of these systems intuitive? Is the answer to bad traffic really more roads? Many of these systems have moved online, supposedly, to ease congestion, but even then, it is only an imposed order. For example, someone I know, who had just turned sixty, was about to apply for government benefits. She traveled to the office, only to be told that she had to apply for it online and then visit the office to submit forms. The bizarre process does not consider that many older people have difficulty with new technology; besides, not everyone has access to technology. If it is online, why not make the process fully online? I have experienced a similar thing when I tried to open a bank account. I was told to sign up online and then visit the bank, which I did, but when I went there, they were offline, so they could not access my account. I asked them whether we could do it manually, as we used to do before modernizing, but they said they have moved fully online, to which I asked, "Then why do I have to physically visit your bank?" I have experienced this odd circular process in other places too, and one of the inconveniences of many offices is that they might ask you to come back multiple times. Add this to the difficulty and expense of commuting in the metro.

I am not sharing this only to whine, but to give examples of how unintuitive systems are forced just to match with "international standards." If the narrow view of modernization is simply moving online, then it creates even more difficulties. The problem is not with the modernization but with the intuitiveness of these processes. What, then, works for the people? We ask the people. We use the languages we speak in. We come from the people's experiences and build a world that makes it easier for us to be who we are. I am not speaking ideally; I am speaking practically.

Decolonization as Authenticity

Decolonization is not just an act of regression. Decolonization is the act of removing the costume we were made to wear by others. Decolonization is being comfortable with our skin; it is interacting naturally with the world around us. It is very true that colonial systems persist today and cause many of our difficulties. After all, these systems were built for the ease of a specific demographic—usually the ruling class and colonial invaders. It is wonderful that we are growing in cultural consciousness and giving our own multiethnic heritage its deserved appreciation and representation. However, focusing only on discerning which symbols and technologies to use or discard by aesthetic preference alone is insufficient. One can, for instance, be fluent in any of the hundred Filipino languages, wear gorgeous ethnic patterns, and have great tattoos, but without an authentic transformation of the inner self (pagbabagong-loob), it is only tokenism, or worse, appropriation. Remember that the early missionaries learned our language to better indoctrinate us with their religious ideologies.

In my view, decolonization could be a journey toward greater authenticity, by placing people in their appropriate context rather than appropriate a one-size-fits-all archetype of cultural aesthetics. Decolonization could mean working to create systems that work for the ordinary Filipino, rather than further inconvenience them—for example, better public transportation and social services. Decolonization could mean the preservation and study of collective memory—as Zeus Salazar suggested, we can approach history in a way that it is written to enrich our ways of knowing, rather than curated for others to see.[13] Decolonization could mean adapting to the tastes and preferences we have rather than making aesthetic choices because it looks "more Filipino." As Leonardo Mercado said, modernization does not necessarily have to mean Westernization. Rather, it is improvement of our sociocultural technology (for example, tools for communication) for our own ease and efficiency—intuitively aligned with our own contexts and cultural tendencies.[14]

In summary, rather than simply rejecting anything "foreign" or cherry-picking what is more "ethnic," decolonization could be a critical approach to challenging prevailing systems that are oppressive (or, at the very least, incredibly inconvenient) in the present, not merely in some romanticized archetypal past. It is a process toward greater authenticity.

-

CHAPTER SEVEN

Deep Spirituality

When the explorer Ferdinand Magellan arrived in the archipelago in 1521, he was depicted by his chronicler as a man of strong conviction who carried an inspired faith. Antonio Pigafetta, Magellan's chronicler, wrote that the naive natives of Cebu were awestruck by the spiritual eloquence that Magellan possessed. Pigafetta wrote that it was through his charisma that he was able to baptize them. But we can also see in Pigafetta's writing how practical our ancestors were—reading between the lines, it is clear their main motivation for accepting Christianity was Magellan's promised armor and weapons.[1] It just so happens that during this time, Cebu's ruler, Rajah Humabon, had political ambitions, and he saw this as a fantastic opportunity to create a military alliance. He was thus baptized as "Don Carlos," and his wife as "Juana." Juana was gifted the Santo Niño, a statue of the child Jesus, which has become, and remains until today, the quintessential symbol of the Philippine Christian faith.

Magellan thus got caught in a political war between Humabon and the ruler of the nearby island of Mactan, Lapu-Lapu. So, with his pride about his supposed military superiority, Magellan went to Mactan to seek their allegiance to the King of Spain, but Lapu-Lapu replied that he did not fear either of them, and that they were ready with their bamboo lances, hardened in fire.[2] The shallow waters did not allow Magellan's cannons to reach the natives on the shore, so they waded in the water, only to be met by the fury of a thousand warriors. They noticed that Magellan was the leader of the party, so they concentrated their forces, eventually piercing him with a lance—after which the other warriors jumped in to slay him. His men, fleeing, were also massacred by the natives.

Magellan's slave, Enrique, was promised freedom once his master died, but Pigafetta informed him that he would continue to be the slave of Magellan's wife. Angered, Enrique told Humabon that the foreigners were about to leave and that he should grab this opportunity to take their ships and items. Humabon invited the two new commanders ashore for a feast, but eventually, his true intentions became clear, and many of the Spaniards were killed. One of the commanders was able to escape, only to suffer the trauma of war and death as he wandered the archipelago aimlessly with increasingly restless and hungry men.[3]

When news of Magellan's ill-fated voyage reached Spain, another expedition was sent. Forty-four years later, the conquistador Miguel López de Legazpi returned to find that the Santo Niño de Cebu had become an important member of the animist pantheon, standing alongside carvings of other native deities.[4] This was seen as an omen of God's approval of Legazpi's campaign, but to the Cebuano natives, the image had already taken a different, more grounded meaning. The Santo Niño de Cebu had become a rain god venerated by the locals and pilgrims from surrounding islands—Nick Joaquin considered it to be our last and greatest pagan deity and a surviving symbol of pre-Hispanic beliefs.[5]

Religion and Society

The Philippines today is a predominantly Catholic country, yet the practices are still deeply animist. The Catholic saints carry the function of the ancient anito. Thousands of people attend the transfer of the statue of Hesus Nazareno, which occurs every January in Quiapo City. It is said that the statue has miraculous properties—one need only touch it, or wipe a towel on it, to receive its blessings. Many people also have their cars blessed in Antipolo City, to receive the protection of Our Lady of Peace and Good Voyage. If you were to enter a Filipino home or office, you may observe a variety of religious symbols. There may be a Bagua mirror on the doorframe to welcome luck as well as other feng shui charms in auspicious areas. There may be a statue of Santo Niño, the child Jesus, which, as I described earlier in the chapter, is a very popular symbol that goes all the way back to the first arrival of the Spaniards. We seem to have a fondness for this divine child, and many treat it as their own, dressing it up in various uniforms. There is a special amulet that is a tiny naked Santo Niño as well, said to be good for business. There is also a variation of the Santo Niño that holds a bag of gold. This is not traditionally Christian, but that does not matter. It is believed to bring prosperity anyway. On the windows, there may be small containers with salt to ward off the *aswang*, a shape-shifting monster in local folklore. All this may be interpreted as syncretic, which implies various "pure" traditions that come together seamlessly. I suppose that makes sense if we can think of these traditions as colorful threads that are turned into a magnificent tapestry. But it would make more sense to say that we make no distinction between sources of power: We use what we believe would work, regardless of where they come from. In other words, we are aware that there is some kind of spiritual reality, and we just use whatever symbol makes sense to us in order to access its grace.

Many of us feel some sort of way about Catholicism. Some consider it antithetical to cultural liberation, being that it was a colonial import. Others see it as a potential path toward true neighborliness—we mean this in the biblical sense, how the Gospels taught that we ought to love our enemies and neighbors as we love ourselves. This is compatible with our cultural values. When discussing the current indigenous worldview, we cannot avoid talking about spirituality because it is so ingrained in the culture. The psychologist Violeta Villaroman-Bautista recommended that the study of local spirituality can be a creative way to approach a culture's intuitive interpretations of reality.[6] In our critical assessment of everyday spirituality as an approach to the indigenous worldview, we do not have to question the faith of millions of Filipinos—but we can wonder what makes a foreign religion so resonant among traditionally animist people. If you recall, this is what Zeus Salazar called the psycho-medical approach, which implies that precolonial spirituality has persisted until today, but has transformed through time.[7] To do this, we must first take a step back from our own biases and really listen to how people practice their faith. That is when we will be able to see that, on a practical level, Philippine Catholicism, like any system of symbols and rituals, is just another way to express shared mystical truths.

Childhood Beliefs

In my grandfather's old house, there was a dark hallway of books on religion, pop psychology, and psychic experiments. At the end of the hallway was a mirror. A priest who claimed to have the ability to "see" said that this hallway was a portal to the spirit world. My childhood was spent reading my grandfather's books. That is where my interest in magic and mythology began. Perhaps the reason I resonated so deeply with those stories of the supernatural is because they were a part of my everyday reality from an early age. I know many people who claim to have the ability to sense the presence of spirits—sometimes, a friend might point to an empty corner of a room and say ominously, "There's a little child there." Different people might have similar experiences in old or abandoned buildings. Since I studied in Catholic schools from elementary to university, we were required to attend religious retreats in quiet houses, far away from the city. Every local school campus and retreat house I have gone to has a resident ghost. I would sometimes speak to the night guards, and they would tell me about disembodied laughter or the sound of someone's footsteps, even when nothing appeared on the security camera. Many people I know have also been taken to a folk healer when they were children, usually after the doctor's recommendations did not seem to work. I also know some people who believe they have been courted by invisible beings from folklore. In my judgment, all these people are functional and relatively sane. The supernatural, at least in our culture, is not so bizarre that it takes us out of our daily lives. It is a natural part of our life, an ordinary topic of our everyday conversations.

I grew up with my mother's folk wisdom. Whenever she bites her tongue, she immediately asks for a number. Then she counts which letter this number lands on. She says that whenever a person bites their tongue accidentally, someone somewhere is talking about them. The letter represents their name. When a utensil falls, she says, "Oh, it looks like we will have a visitor soon." Whenever we enter a house, she tells me to count the steps. "Count like this: *oro, plata, mata.* Gold, silver, death. See if it lands on *mata.*" One night, after watching a scary movie, I asked her how safe we would be in our house if the monster from the movie was real. She comforted me and said, "Do not worry. There are religious medals in the foundation and pillars of this house." These are all supernatural beliefs, and my mother is a very religious person. I would say that there is a difference between someone who is religious and someone who is superstitious, although I am sure that many secular folk would lump them together. But if the basic idea of what we call superstitious beliefs are just practices that do not seem to do anything protective or productive, then even religionists will be able to identify practices that they consider to be superstition, compared to their own beliefs, which, to them, absolutely work. (To the secular-minded, none of these beliefs seem to work anyway, so perhaps to them, the identification of religion versus superstition will not make any difference.) The ritual practice of religion, I think, serves an important personal function: that is, to structure one's consciousness and time in a way that makes the larger world somewhat manageable. In any case, what I want to point out here is not that my mother dabbles in superstitions, but that they do not seem to clash with her traditional religious beliefs at all.

Whenever I would disobey my elders or waste my dinner, my mother would warn me of *gaba.* I have always imagined gaba to be like a bad stomachache. Later, I would learn that gaba is believed to be the punishment for a moral offense. It can manifest as anything. For example, a natural disaster that destroys a town might be interpreted as gaba because the townsfolk kept throwing their trash in the nearby river. Gaba implies that we are part of a cosmic system, an ecology of self, nature, and community. This concept is, apparently, uniquely Visayan, because when I brought it up with my Tagalog friends, they did not understand it. After describing it to them, they said, "Oh, so it is like karma?" I know that they mean karma in the sense that something is a divine punishment—not in the actual religious sense of this term.

My friends and teachers taught me other things. I was told never to point at ancient trees because it was rude to the spirits that lived there. In the case I do accidentally point, they said I should bite my finger. Perhaps this is also why many Filipinos still point with their lips instead. When crossing grassy areas, even if just a garden, I was told to always ask for permission from the spirits, so that I do not accidentally step on them. I was taught to say, *"Tabi tabi po"* (Excuse me, please step aside, I am coming through). This seems to reflect an intuitive and sustainable relationship with nature. Dirt mounds are said to be the home of *nuno*, who is an old man with a long beard and a pointy hat. The word *nuno*, I learned, is short for *ninuno*, which means "ancestor." It is believed that, when a person passes away, their spirit returns to nature. Sometimes, dead relatives might visit us as butterflies or birds; they might rest on an item that used to belong to the person when they were alive, such as their pillow. This is called *paramdam*, which refers to when someone is making themselves felt. Once we have forgotten the names of our ancestors, they become nameless nature spirits. All these spirits are called anito. I have always known anito as the wooden carvings of people sitting with their knees up and their arms crossed. Each of these carvings represents a soul. Many people seem to think that we worship our ancestors in the same way people worship deities. But it is more like a negotiation. This extends to modern practice, where a person might make a promise *(panata)* to a saint that they would do something or go on a pilgrimage in their name if only they would grant a favor.

For as long as I remember, I have feared folk horror. I cannot fully explain the intuitive, visceral, low-grade terror I often experience just walking around areas that feel highly charged with animist forces. I have also been somewhat hesitant to meet folk healers. My Catholic upbringing never ignored the potential of folk magic—it only ever warned me of the spiritual dangers that awaited. It is not that spirits are inherently dangerous, but that they are strangers. And, because we do not know who they are or what their intentions may be, they might manipulate and hurt us. This, I think, is less a demonization of cultural practices and more practical spiritual advice. It would seem that many of those who approach any world spirituality with a full but ignorant openness are in it for the cultural aesthetic rather than the underlying philosophy or the metaphysical potential of ritual. Anyone whose practice is deep and focused would warn of the real psychospiritual dangers: madness, spiritual possession, oppressive and incessant disturbing thoughts or nightmares, and hallucinations or apparitions. In the field of transpersonal psychology, this is called a "spiritual emergency," which involves perceptual, cognitive, and psychosomatic changes in functioning without the presence of a biological disease.[8] Unlike our traditional understanding of mental illness as a dysfunction, spiritual emergencies are not always negative: sometimes, they are perceived by the individual as an initiation to spiritual awakening. Again, that does not mean that one should enter without care, like the colonial adventurers of old when they blazed through strange lands—to be appropriately guided into the mysteries, one should enter with respect and humility, and a willingness to truly understand.

The Surwano

During the Holy Week break in 2024, I flew to my hometown in Negros Island to spend time with my family. We stayed at my grandfather's house in Silay. My mother informed me that someone from the nearby farm has a cousin who is a *surwano* (folk practitioner). "If you want," she said, "you can interview her as part of your research." She was interested in sitting in and asking her own questions—so was my sister, cousin, and grandfather. At the time, my uncle, a Catholic priest, was staying in the house, but he opted to stay upstairs so that the surwano would not feel uncomfortable with his presence. Since my ability to speak and understand Hiligaynon is limited, my mother and cousin offered to help in translating.

Although I prepared some basic questions, I did not think of this as an interview in the traditional sense. It would be a *kuwentuhan* (sharing of stories), where the researcher (me) does not simply extract information. Rather, the researcher participates in an equal exchange of ideas. In any case, I just wanted to learn more about local beliefs and practices, beyond the books and papers I have read on them. Through my mother's contact, we asked the surwano for permission to record our conversation, and for me to share what I learned. This follows the indigenous research method of having a bridge, or tulay, as an intermediary to coordinate with a potential informant—in a culture that values relationships, having a tulay shows the trustworthiness of the outsider who is interested in learning the local customs. The surwano responded that she was all right with it, as long as the recording would not be visual. She said this was because she did not want people to think that she was selling her knowledge.

Our informant arrived a few hours later. It was fortuitous that we met on a Tuesday, because she was going to travel far away the next day to meet with other surwanos. Holy Week is an important time for them because this is when they get their special medicine. Tuesday is also a good day, she said, because things are "clearer." We settled down and I explained that I teach at a university and that I wanted to be more familiar with the topics I teach. I once again asked for her permission if I could record through audio only and eventually share the contents of our conversation with others. I assured her that nobody would know her identity.

She said yes to all this and added that it was important for people to know what her work truly is about rather than making assumptions.

I approach this topic with careful and respectful skepticism. During our meeting, it was not my position to challenge her, only to learn from her, but I interpret these experiences now through my own ways of knowing. That said, this is not a generalization of all folk practitioners, nor is it an investigation meant to disprove the surwano's worldview in light of other worldviews. I am not a medical doctor, so I have no opinions on the veracity of her medical claims. I hope we can avoid romanticizing indigenous folk healing or setting it against modern science—the surwano herself said that there is no such dichotomy, even in her practice. "Go to the doctor first," she said. "Only come to me for a second opinion."

To begin with, our informant told us that each practitioner is different depending on their personal beliefs and expertise—a babaylan, she said, is a kind of surwano.* The term *surwano*, therefore, is used here as an umbrella term to refer to Filipino folk practitioners, in the same way that the pediatrician, surgeon, and psychiatrist are kinds of doctors, or perhaps more accurately in the way that professors with doctorate degrees each have their own niches yet are all called "doctor." Of course, local practice does not have the same institutional standardization, but we do not have to insist on either specificity or generalization. Although there are different names and different specific practices in various places in the country, they are all understood intuitively. What I have noticed is that various terms for folk practitioners are often used out of convenience, particularly when referring to certain practices. But it seems that the practitioners themselves do not seem to mind, if we know what we are talking about. It is an entirely different issue when, in the academic setting, we try to distinguish between the babaylan, *albularyo* (herbalist), and *mangkukulam* (witch). Our informant said that all who use

---

* The term *babaylan* is generally used to refer to the Philippine shaman, but it is actually the Visayan practitioner in particular. There are other names across the archipelago.

supernatural powers for whatever purpose, regardless of whether they are used for healing or harming, regardless of whether they are done with spirits or saints, are called surwano.

She claimed that her powers are directly from God the Father. She said that she used to be *dungol* (mischievous) because she often hung out with boys. Nobody would believe that she would ever become a surwano. When her husband got sick and the doctors could not explain it, he went to a surwano and came home with his strength regained. He was showing off to her that he could carry heavy things again. He promised to give back to the community by becoming a surwano, and eventually, many people came to him for healing. The sessions involved wiping the patient's body with a towel, and it made him uncomfortable whenever he would have to do it to women. His wife, our informant, offered to help him. Since he was the provider of the household, he still had to work, and it became difficult when he would have to rush back home to heal a patient. So, his wife, who learned by watching him, took over. That is how she started.

When a patient still feels discomfort, despite all their medical tests coming back normal, they might go to the surwano; the sickness may be something else. Our informant called it *"halit,"* which in Hiligaynon refers to something bad that happens, such as a natural disaster. I asked if it was the same as *kulam* or *barang,* which are usually translated as "witchcraft" or "sorcery," but she just told me that anything harmful is halit. Halit is caused by intention, or *pulong,* even if a person is not a surwano. Envy can cause halit. It moves like a message on a thread directed at a recipient, and once it arrives, it may manifest in different ways. The cause of death may be a heart attack, dehydration, or another medical emergency, but the surwano would know that it was halit. "There will come a time that people no longer need weapons to kill," she said. "Intention will be enough." Her practice is to return the halit to its sender. This is called balik (literally meaning "return").

Some surwanos, she said, might be blinded by the allure of money, and they may charge ridiculous amounts. They might say, for example, that the patient needs to light a particular candle for a week, and then they would overcharge for that one candle. Our informant said that she knew of someone who spent almost all her earnings from working abroad on a corrupt surwano. These sketchy practitioners, she said, are also willing to harm others for a price. She admitted that she has also been invited by wealthy people to cause halit to their opponents. They would tell her to name whatever price, but she would always clarify that she is not that kind of surwano. Those surwanos have to protect themselves because if their victim goes to another surwano and the halit is returned, they will die. Otherwise, this bounces off them and goes to the one who requested the service, and their family gets cursed until their lineage ends. Our informant said that the bad surwano is like metal: strong at first, but more exposure to the sun and rain makes them rust until they become useless. It reminds me of the old saying, *Walang sumisira sa bakal kundi ang sarili nitong kalawang.* (Nothing destroys metal except its own rust.) There is no other name for those who cause harm: They are still surwano.

Other Practitioners

The great folklorist Francisco Demetrio distinguished between the shaman and the witch. Whereas the shaman worked toward order and community, the witch worked toward disorder and individuality.[9] These, he said, were two fundamental ways we deal with psycho-mystical realities. Today, we believe that the mangkukulam is a witch in the fairy-tale sense, and this is shown in local movies. Alongside the feminist reclamation of the European witch as a symbol of the oppression of women, many Filipino advocates insist that the mangkukulam was a once respected figure demonized by the Spanish colonizers. Similarly, the precolonial babaylan (traditionally a woman or a man in women's clothing) has also become the archetype used by modern advocates of the decolonization of gender. The ethnomusicologist and cultural worker Grace Nono posed the question of who this movement is meant to empower, since the babaylan tradition was never actually lost despite centuries of colonization.[10] Contemporary babaylans have thus far been excluded in what Nono pointed out to be a largely urban, middle-class, and Westernized movement. I have also seen some younger people use the aesthetics of the babaylan or mangkukulam to localize their Wiccan practice. In our efforts to honor the indigenous, we categorize endlessly, gate-keep cultural traditions, and wear culture like a costume. In contrast, our conversation with the surwano had an intuitive simplicity. There was no intricate jargon: All the terms she used were terms of convenience (or literally what certain things are called). The practitioner is called a surwano. They heal halit by returning it (balik). Her worldview is easy to understand and can be summarized in two points:

1. The power to heal and to harm are gifts from a divine source; we are just instruments.

2. All things are interconnected and bound by mutual intention.

When I was younger, we spent most of our Sundays in San Juan having lunch with other family members. The owner of the house in San Juan is a faith healer, whose healing ministry began in the early 1990s. She would do it freely without expecting payment, especially since she sees her ability as a gift from God. On her altar sat a statue of Mary, Mediatrix of All Grace, the supposedly miraculous apparition that occurred in a Carmelite monastery in Lipa, Batangas. It was already ruled as "non-supernatural" in 1951; this was reaffirmed in 2015. Nevertheless, devotees still report miracles. "Patients" would sit down in front of this faith healer's statue, and she would put them into a trance by repeating the prayer "Come Holy Spirit." Her palms would heat whenever she would conduct her sessions—something that also occurred with the surwano I met. I have seen people speak in tongues, and I have heard stories of cancer cases that went into remission. By the definition of our informant, this faith healer, though Catholic, is also a surwano.

Our informant also works with saints—or more specifically, statues of the saints. She said that it did not matter which saint it was, as long as the surwano treated them like family. Whenever she would leave the house, for example, she would let them know. She said that people would not dare enter her house when she was away because they would see the guardians sitting on the stairs or watching by the doorway. The saints are like children, she said, whom you need to feed so that they would grow. They would also lose potency if you do not take care of them right. This is not the same treatment that Catholics have for these religious images. In Catholic belief, statues of the saints should just be reflections of divinity, in the same way that a picture of a loved one is not the loved one per se but a reminder of them. Idolatry is worshiping the images rather than what they represent. But we cannot say that the surwano is worshiping these statues in the way one would worship a god. The statues have power as they are, and our informant said that it does not matter which saint they were. (However, there seems to be a preference for the Santo Niño, the child Jesus, since, as I mentioned earlier, it can be cared for as one would an actual child.) They are not "gods" but supernatural helpers.

Interpreting Supernatural Phenomena

The surwano also said that there was a mother and a child in the house we were in. They supposedly lived on the land before the house was built. She said that they would not harm us if they were not disturbed either. Interestingly, when I first entered the house, I did see what may have been the shadow of a child running, but it may have also just been a trick of the light. The maids at the time had also reported the sound of wailing at night. There were also strange knocks on the door and no one waiting outside. My partner stayed in the house for a month. One afternoon, as I was seated on a couch outside her room, she opened the door, looked at me, and asked me what I needed. I was confused and she asked why I knocked on her door. I told her that nobody knocked on her door.

One night, I heard the wailing and followed it. It turned out just to be the wind, whistling through a window. The house has wide windows, and it is often pleasantly windy. This would also explain the knocking, which may have just been doors rattling due to the breeze. What is interesting, however, is that my grandmother, who has been bedridden for a while, could "see" a child and their mother. She would sometimes tell her nurse to ask the child to come closer. Then again, this could just be the dreams of an older woman, reminiscing about her earlier days as a young mother. The surwano may have already heard about all of this before coming to meet us and then just confirmed it for us. It is, after all, a small town, and word gets spread quickly. Otherwise, we will have to actually investigate the paranormal reality of shared visions.

After our conversation, we thanked her. I offered her some money for her time. It would also be my contribution to her travel expenses for her upcoming pilgrimage. She did not ask for any payment, nor did she seem to expect it, so I had to tell her that the money was a "donation." She accepted it and left.

Felt Religion

I have always assumed that there is a difference between cognitive and felt religion. The former imposes order through legalistic dogma. It insists on reality through logical argument and promotes hierarchies that facilitate social control. It tends to weaponize guilt. The latter is experienced as a visceral reality. It bypasses reason, yet it is accepted as true, in the same way dreams feel real when we are in them. Dream imagery still requires interpretation to be intelligible and meaningful to the waking mind, and so we adopt the symbols accessible to us. In our case, we use Catholicism. Many of us who have experienced Catholicism as a cognitive religion can be unconvinced of its arguments. It is easy to see that, beneath its grandiose pretensions of humility and honor, the church can be very human and very fallible. For the most part, it has distanced itself from its true purpose: that of unity with the divine, on the most visceral and organic level of being One Body. As the philosopher Alan Watts observed, the churches today are monarchical courts, drawing from the ancient political system that involves subjugation to a king—and in our case, the King of Kings, who is above everything and is far, far away.[11] Protestant churches, he noticed, were modeled after judicial courts. This shows how much we have lost the meaningful essence of ritual and mythology, especially in our institutional religions, by further imposing the hierarchical kaniya-kaniya mentality onto an aspect of the human experience supposedly designed to allow us to meet God in our lives and bring the Kingdom of Heaven to us. That is not to say that we should remove all intellectual attempts to grasp the divine. This is a fantastic way to approach transcendent mysteries, but I think, in this field, it should operate more as a method rather than an end in and of itself. In other words, we can approach spiritual experience through cognitive efforts via overstimulation toward gnostic revelation, but we often stop at pedantic legalism. In the end, therefore, priests and judges have the same essential duty: that is to assess the law and condemn violators.

Corruption and abuse are human problems, and this is where mystical teachings and actual practices diverge. When religion is used as a political tool to oppress others, it is no longer what it was meant to be. If we are to judge a religion, we must instead look to their saints and great teachers, and there we will see how they stood with the vulnerable and fought for prosocial values until their death. We will also see that many of these saints were also mystics. Felt religion, therefore, is the religion that cognitive religion approximates. So, when we work with Catholic symbolism, we are using it like a language. It does not seem to matter what spiritual language you are using as long as it makes sense to you and to the people you are sharing it with. What is more valuable is the mystical reality that flows beneath these symbols. Watts said that we can approach ritual and symbolism through a sense of play. Imagine yourself as an omnipotent being who knows all things and can do everything.

Nothing can surprise you at all unless you can hide from yourself some-how. All of this, then, is a game of hide-and-seek.[12] An ancient Hindu saying, *tat tvam asi* (that thou art), implies that you are a fragmentary manifestation of shared, absolute reality. Watts translates it beautifully as "You are it," in the sense that you are it, the one playing the game, and you are it, the one playing tag, tasked to chase after everyone else, who, incidentally, is also you.[13] This should not enhance our spiritual narcis-sism, but rather encourage our groundedness in, and our participation with, the world around us.

Perhaps what most surprised me about our conversation with the sur-wano was that her beliefs did not surprise me. Maybe I entered with the hope that I would learn something new. I am nevertheless pleased that the existing ethnographic literature is consistent with current practice. This is despite most book-length studies on the matter being somewhat outdated and tragically out of print. There are newer studies too, but nothing much has changed. Much of what she said was, at least to me, intuitively understood—I suspect that this may be why it is so easy for her patients to understand her framework. It is already embedded in our culture.

There was also a portion during our meeting where we all had our palms and faces read by her. She looked at my palm and told me my for-tune, claiming that it was to be my destiny, written from when I was born. Yet, later, she told the others that the readings she gave were just "guides" and that it is still up to us how it goes. She also said that it was possible to alter my fate by changing the markings under a full moon. When I debriefed with my family, we started filling in the gaps of what the sur-wano said, reinterpreting her readings to fit the closest possibility. But if she really knew all this, she would have been the one to say it. It was then that I realized that what she did to us was a form of "cold reading," something that horoscope writers, mediums, and mentalists do to make their target feel like they are being uniquely read when the statements they make are vague enough to be interpreted correctly. This has little to do specifically with Filipino culture and more to do with our human tendency to find meaning in the world.

The surwano's practice—wherever they are across the archipelago—is a fascinating manifestation of the intuitive worldview of most Filipinos. The invisible beings and magical forces that are ever-present in our culture are psychic symbols that bridge the gap between the material and the mystical. These are deep realities, echoes of ancestral memory.

CHAPTER EIGHT

-

Personal Liberation

We can see that the systems we are forced to navigate today were probably born out of some practical human necessity. For example, maybe our tendency to hoard resources comes from our ancestors' need to insure ourselves against unpredictable climates; this ended up becoming a system that promoted the mindless accumulation of wealth, often at the expense of others. Maybe, at least psychologically speaking, consumerism is rooted in our real need to survive, and now, the fear of missing out (FOMO) is just the primal terror of losing access to resources. Many of us still struggle with problems of survival: whether or not a struggling worker will be able to feed their family, if a parent will see their child after fleeing a war zone, or whether a homeless person will die first of hunger or disease. The rest of us are concerned with artificial problems, often created by companies to sell products that may not be necessary for our physical survival, but useful for social survival. This means the latest fashion trends, gadgets, apps, and so on. That is not to say that artificial problems are *not* problems, nor would I want to engage in any comparison of "who has it worse." I am only pointing out the strange situation we are in: Artificial problems can feel just as real as concerns for our self-preservation—precisely because that feeling touches on some primal tendency within us to keep ourselves alive. It is interesting, for example, that we have terms like *social suicide* to refer to nonphysical death that can be just as terrifying as physical death. It is tempting to minimize these concerns when faced with the realities of war and the climate crisis, but comparison would only make us feel better, in the same way a child would be guilted into finishing a meal because there are starving children somewhere in the world. Someone being forced to finish their food will not automatically feed others who are hungry (most especially those halfway around the world), and one could even argue that the person who finished their food took resources away from those who need it. Today, there is too much food waste from places where people can eat comfortably, which shows that it may be possible to feed more people if it were to be shared in some way. In any case, once basic needs are met, we may begin to concern ourselves with other human needs—and thus even artificial and social needs become part of our development.

The psychologist Abraham Maslow, one of the pioneers in the humanistic psychology field, theorized that we are motivated to fulfill the biological, psychological, and social homeostasis of our being.[1] Maslow's hierarchy of needs is a fundamental concept in mainstream psychology. Once we are assured that certain needs are, and will be, consistently met, we seek other assurances that round out our sense of stability in the world. It is, of course, quite possible for a person to feel fulfilled despite lacking in certain aspects. A person can be happy despite poverty and find meaning outside social relationships. But feeling a threat to our identity if certain intangible needs are not met makes sense—such as the need for belongingness and esteem. A need more basic than the need to be recognized is the need to feel seen.

We know that when needs go unfulfilled, we die. Without the biological needs of food, water, or life-saving medicine, we die a bodily death; without the security of houses and gates, we are exposed to dangers both natural and human; without meaningful relationships, we lose access to social resources; without recognition, we die a spiritual death. Our evolution as human beings necessitates our adaptation to physical and social elements: We have developed technologies to improve the production and maintenance of resources and protect us against invaders and most natural disasters. The fulfillment of our needs today is tied to this context. We know that most systems were made to satisfy the needs of particular groups of people, but maybe even the most well-meaning colonizer (if there is such a thing) intended that "primitive" civilizations should be taught their "modern" ways to survive as members of the human species. In fact, this was the rhetoric used by the United States during their colonial rule in the Philippines: that they would introduce "modern civilization" to those who were not killed in the Philippine-American War. American education, taught in American English, in US-built schools, served to propagate American values. At the time, the condition placed on us in order to gain independence was that we would have learned how to "self-govern"—that is, in the American way.[2]

But we also know that certain techniques and ways of living are just not useful in certain environments—for example, thick jackets that are useful in wintry weather are impractical in tropical heat. We are quick to adapt, but if these new technologies are useless to us, there really is no other reason why we should continue to use them—except, of course, to satisfy foreign standards, which we consider to be wiser than our own intuition. It is strange, then, that despite our apparent independence, we still look to outsiders (that is, former colonial masters) for guidance, like a monkey asking a bird how they got to the branches. The bird will say, "Just use your wings!" And the monkey will scrounge about to find the sturdiest leaves in the jungle to construct wings, failing many times; and when it does get to the branch, it wobbles because it sits awkwardly like a bird, falling again and again. There are two lessons here: first is that the monkey could have just climbed up, and the second is that, despite the monkey failing, they now have more knowledge about the jungle than the bird does. Here is a third lesson: at least the monkey attempted it, because, sometimes, we find ourselves still waiting at the foot of the tree.

The Kaniya-Kaniya Society

The kaniya-kaniya (to each their own) society prioritizes individual success through disciplined effort. In this system, success would lead to status, and status gives a person access to luxury and comfort—ideally, these should be beyond what an individual needs. Status symbols should be symbols of exclusivity and indications not just of wealth, but of one's drive to succeed in the kaniya-kaniya system. Then, prosperity is the outcome of being "moral" in a system whose values include persistence and adventurousness. In truth, having some kind of status is also necessary to survive. We know this because those who have no status—or have supposedly ruined themselves—are shunned. They are the marginalized groups of society, those who, for whatever reason, have difficulty achieving success in the kaniya-kaniya system.

In a kaniya-kaniya system, one's worth or value is determined by their profitability. Attaining success is dependent on how productive they are and how comfortably they can consume. You must offer something unique to the world or be exceptional at what you do. Mastery in a field makes you necessary, and if you are needed somewhere, then you will be given many things just to stay there—until you have been fully exploited—when everyone knows how to do the skill you've excelled at, or when new technology renders your skill set obsolete. You cannot exploit something useless. Some might create a need where there is none so that demand for it increases—and if you are the only one who can offer it, you earn status, such as with artificial needs. On a more personal level, you are expected to be a finished product all by yourself, which is why we have statements like, "You cannot love others if you do not know how to love yourself," implying that you must be complete before you can offer anything to others. Being incomplete—that is, being "disabled" in one way or another—lowers your value in a society biased toward the able-bodied. Those without status are "nobodies," invisible to the provident eyes of society. The loss of status, through disability, but also other things, such as scandal, can be terrible: homelessness, poverty, and maybe even the deprivation of liberty through incarceration.

The problem is that, as the ancient philosopher Epictetus said, you can only truly control your thoughts, perceptions, and your will to act—everything else is beyond your control, and depending too much on things you cannot control can cause you too much grief.[3] This truth is still relevant today, even though we have been fooled into thinking we can control *everything*. So many things vital to our survival are totally outside our control—on a personal level, we cannot anticipate the sudden onset of war, disaster, pandemics, or economic crises. We cannot expect sudden technological advancements that make our jobs obsolete. It seems that our fear of losing jobs to new technology says a lot about how many jobs are greatly mechanical. Of course, this is not to degrade those who work repetitive jobs, because, like anyone else, they deserve humane treatment and livable compensation—perhaps even more so for jobs that require the full use of one's body and spirit. Technology taking over our most tedious work could ideally give us space to pursue other passions: art, love, travel, and the pursuit of knowledge. Better technology could allow us to enjoy different forms of leisure. I wonder, then, whether there is a level of technology that is only necessary to live a comfortable life, beyond which technology becomes superfluous and imaginary. But these days, as technology becomes more complex, we are forced to adapt and specialize, over again, because we need to be relevant and useful in a system that treats us like products. We are, oddly, competing with technology, which has no need for the benefits of status, yet technology is making it more difficult for the everyday person to attain it. Thus, the fear of losing status, and therefore losing access to resources, despite our best efforts, can cause incredible anxiety—what philosopher Alain de Botton aptly called "status anxiety."[4]

The kaniya-kaniya system has persisted for a long time, and it will likely persist on, despite monumental historical revolutions that have happened in different parts of the world, despite libraries of academic dissertations on how to build better and more inclusive societies, despite activists and allies speaking up and organizing protests both on the ground and online. We know there is something awfully flawed with it, but we continue to participate and dream of ways to succeed. Maybe, then, the kaniya-kaniya mentality is a natural human tendency—that is, part of human nature. But that we can say so much about it also implies that we know we can hope for an alternative to it, or at the very least, a way to make it more humane.

Mental Health

Modern kaniya-kaniya societies might recognize that the well-being of individuals is important—if only as functioning parts of a machine that needs to keep going. In this sense, the psychiatrist is a mechanic, and therapy is periodic maintenance. The system remains unquestioned; we think that just because we were born into a world that already existed, how it is going now is how it has always been and how it must always be. Then, individual difficulty in this system is an individual problem, a kind of defect or fluke in an otherwise fully operational system. We see this in the stigma associated with disability, particularly disability that is perceived to be within one's control, such as addiction ("Stop using it if you know that it is bad for you") or depression ("Just think happy thoughts" or "Get over it"). We often recommend taking responsibility for one's well-being ("If you cannot care for yourself, how can you care for others?") and, if necessary, cutting off "toxic" people who are preventing us from achieving our personal goals. For serious cases, all kinds of medication could numb certain effects so that one could function properly in society. Although medication can be helpful with professional guidance, it does not by itself address the issues surrounding one's condition, nor does it identify and take out the root of harmful behavior. The mainstream idea of the self, drawn mainly from the early psychoanalysts, is that we all have, within each of us, a shadowy, primordial, animalistic space that influences our behaviors and attitudes—what we call the "unconscious mind." This space absorbs our life experiences, and if we go through something traumatic, its memory is repressed, hidden away—but it continues its clandestine growth, influencing our daily lives. Nothing in the unconscious is "rational," at least judged by the logic of language, and it vents out into the conscious level as disturbing recollections, nightmares, slips of the tongue, and synchronicities. But it is all within. Our repressed traumas, intentional and unintentional, are held in the deepest, most unknown space inside the individual mind. Talk therapy was meant to be cathartic, a way to loosen the pressure before the individual reaches their limit and breaks down. Still, as an individual, it is your duty to recognize your potential issues and seek help for yourself. In the kaniya-kaniya society, you must be mindful of how functional you are as a living product.

The kaniya-kaniya system does offer many therapeutic solutions to personal life problems yet operates with the fundamental belief that everything that happens to an individual is their fault and responsibility. On the one hand, this is very empowering in that it gives us the illusion of control and encourages the idea of meritocracy, that we all get what we deserve based on the effort we put in. On the other hand, your failure and suffering are understood as coming from your lack of discipline, an unwillingness to grovel or take risks, or whatever it is that self-styled life coaches and self-help books claim is the issue. The assumption is that the system is fine; you are just not playing the game right. There are any number of life rules or principles to follow—you will see authors who enjoy listing their advice, following the authoritative tradition of Moses with God's Ten Commandments. If, despite your best personal efforts, you are still unable to succeed, then they will say that there really must be something wrong with your internal machinery. We go back to the idea that the system works, and to be a functioning part of it, you must be of sound mind and body.

Again, we know that many things are outside our control, and that the system was made for a particular type of person (the colonial power or ruling class), ensuring their ease in succeeding. It is easy for the privileged to recommend having big dreams and taking risks when they do not have to worry about affording groceries. It is easy for the privileged to say, "We all have twenty-four hours in a day," when, for the ordinary worker, eight to ten hours and sometimes even more are spent working and four to six hours are spent commuting (especially in Metro Manila traffic, which is horrendous), leaving barely enough time for household chores and sleep—much less to add networking and other streams of income. Add to these societal expectations family expectations, such as what is experienced by many *tagasalo* (catchers) who are expected to work hard to help pay for their siblings' school tuition or care for the elderly in their families. The tagasalo is a part of Filipino family dynamics: They are the child who takes on the most responsibilities in the family. They may have been raised with this reasonability, but most of the time, it is because they feel a sense of duty to care for others, especially if they feel nobody else is stepping up.[5] These children take on quasi-parental roles to ease tensions or ensure family harmony. To them, there may be a sense of power in this dynamic, and even though they would often feel overwhelmed, they would probably not doubt that they are loved, respected, and, most importantly, needed.

Perhaps, if we only thought of ourselves, we could live comfortably. But we do not only live for ourselves—we live for more things beyond us: people, things, and experiences. But given the imposition of a kaniya-kaniya society to succeed alone, by your own effort, beating others to the heights of status—while also managing societal expectations, keeping healthy relationships with family and friends, and personal desires *(luho)*—it is unsurprising that we would be driven mad by it all. When I was younger, and we would see a vagrant in the street muttering to themselves, I would hear whispers, "You know, that person used to be very intelligent." Going mad means being so overwhelmed that one's bait (goodness and sanity) gets broken, and one loses a connection with their own identity (nawala sa sarili). This is most classically represented in Sisa, a character in Jose Rizal's novel *Noli Me Tangere*, who lost her children to the corrupt colonial authority. *Noli* is required reading for us, and I remember, whenever someone would choose to portray Sisa in school performances, it would be as an unkempt woman, crying out, "Crispin! Basilio! My children, where are you?" These days, Sisa would likely be diagnosed as displaying symptoms of schizophrenia, but in those days, and even in folk perception, we understand why she went mad for systemic reasons. A mother whose reality was shaken by a corrupt system, having lost that which has shaped her identity, wandering now, overwhelmed with grief to the point of breaking her bait, knowing no one, not even herself.

In a kaniya-kaniya system, however, it is the other way around: mental illness is said to cause negative life events.* The psychiatrist Thomas Szasz said that "mental illness" is today used as a convenient myth to explain a person's difficulties in life, especially their difficulty functioning in society.[6] If it is not a condition caused by brain damage, "mental illness" is most likely just a diagnosis based on psychosocial expectations of what "normal" should look like. We might then say that certain biological aspects, maybe genetically inherited, can make a person more vulnerable to mental illness, defined here as dysfunction, distressing cognition, and deviant behavior. While this may be true, it implies that there is a narrow societal corridor through which only the "normal" can pass through. The fact that people born differently abled, or even those who become disabled, are vulnerable to threats of joblessness, homelessness, and stigma, already shows that the system serves only a particular type of person. *Dysfunction,* of course, implies function, though we only look at what is "wrong" without critically examining what standards we are using to assess what is "right." Again, "deviant" behavior is just disobedience, defined according to societal norms.

---

* I am talking about our popular understanding; of course there is way more nuance within the field, especially among my colleagues whose work is to study and treat those suffering from personal and systemic conditions. In professional circles, the approach is and has always been largely biopsychosocial, which is to say, holistic.

To be clear, I am not at all minimizing the reality of mental distress. I am only advocating that we recognize the social realities that affect our individual psychologies, and work on improving those conditions. A child has difficulties in school; before rushing to diagnose them with a learning disorder, maybe consider the quality of their home life, the socioeconomic status of their family, and whether they have supportive peers or not. Someone is acting out bizarrely; before punishment and exile become a final consequence of their behavior, and before claiming that they have a personality disorder, maybe ask them why they are doing this, maybe assess their environment, or maybe help them address their traumatic experiences. There is too much reliance on the transactional aspects of the mental health field to address all these concerns and too little acknowledgment of systemic problems that ostracize "abnormal" people. We are more irritable when we are hungry or tired; it takes a lot of effort to focus when we are overwhelmed; we lose track of our priorities when we are stressed. If we can extend the same grace we do to hungry and sleepy people to the "mentally ill," we might find that there are likely very reasonable explanations for why someone is acting in a certain way. But for a kaniya-kaniya society to function seamlessly, there must be no derailments to its processes, so it is no wonder why the old asylums housed all people who deviated from the norm of what we might consider "civilized" folk.

It is wonderful that more people are more open to recommending therapy nowadays. Still, I wonder if this is coming from the rhetoric that we ought to care for ourselves first before caring for others—a kaniya-kaniya trait that tells us we should be finished products. I reiterate my comment about the psychiatrist-mechanic. Even our ways of personal healing, what we call "self-care," tend to be varying forms of self-isolation. This is, of course, different from meaningful and reflective solitude. We are treated as isolated individuals who must, if we are to be "functional," consistently and reliably produce and consume. We are people-as-products, and when we accept that this is what we are, we are held responsible for our own defects. Self-isolation, as a recommended response to being burned out, is a kaniya-kaniya solution, and it prevents the possibility of people coming together to support each other and challenge the system itself. It prioritizes the productivity of an organic being, which is incredibly dehumanizing, considering that even things in nature have their time. An old saying that I am reminded of is, *Ang murang dayap, pigain mo man ay walang katas.* You can squeeze an unripe lime all you want, but it will not produce juice. Why should human beings, being part of nature, and being nature itself, be expected to always be ripe?

Toward Liberation

It seems to me that there are four stages of engaging with a societal system. I hope you forgive me for placing this in what looks like a hierarchical model; it is the simplest way to make a point. Understand, however, that this is not hierarchical in the sense that one follows the other—rather, think of these stages as various psychic landscapes that we can visit, regardless of our social position.

The first is blindly following a system. There is no awareness here. It is what we were born into. "It is what it is," we say. "That is the way the world works." We do not question how the system moves, but we complain about how inefficient most things are. Our life milestones have been set at certain ages. We ought to have done certain things, and we ought to be earning a certain amount. Social and historical contexts do not matter, because one's survival is one's own concern. Self-help books and coaching seminars can empower the person living in this stage; comparison, above and below, gives them a sense of where they are in the hierarchy of society. Those who cannot catch up can feel alienated from their lifestyle: There is a sense of boredom and meaninglessness with tedious routine. The only sense of freedom they feel is on vacation, but even there, their mind operates in preparation for a return to the system.

The second stage is for a select few who know how to work within the system. They have successfully gamified it and might be having fun doing so. They have no further ambition beyond the success they have achieved. Many have no awareness of what gave them an advantage against the competition, which is often socioeconomic privilege or supportive peers. They see their success as their own, and, to those in the first stage, they become the success story. The second stage is filled with rags-to-riches fantasies (so inspiring because they are so rare) of emerging triumphantly from struggle. One can be in this stage despite not being financially successful—if one imagines themselves with certainty to be a wealthy person in the future. The one with *diskarte* (strategies) is commended, but for everyone else, there is a sense of learned helplessness that seems to say, "You can only be successful if you work with the system." Those who claim to break out of the system, of the nine-to-five, are in fact still operating within the system, for their success is measured through social approval. This is the difference between the first and second stages: Many people, sick of the tedium of the first stage, find their own way to play with the system, of finding other streams of income. The promise of becoming your own boss is perhaps the greatest fantasy of this stage. Most psycho-medical interventions operate on this level, where patients are given the skills or medication necessary to be functional members of society.

The third stage is being able to see the system clearly for what it is: a game imposed on us that we can refuse to play, albeit with real consequences. The one who sees the system also sees how it exploits and oppresses others. They are likely to resist and challenge norms and stand up for justice and inclusivity. To be clear, just because a person does not see themselves as part of the system does not necessarily mean they are on this third stage. Their standard is still the system itself, for being an outsider or rogue plays into the adventurous myths of individualism. Regardless, many who enter this third stage also conclude the worst: "If this is all a game, then I am living in a lie." To an existential extreme, one might think that nothing truly matters and that this is all a cosmic illusion. They then slip back into former stages, imagining in vain that Sisyphus is happily rolling the boulder up the mountain, only for it to fall again, for eternity.

The fourth stage is following one's own standards while embracing one's own context and making the most out of one's privileges. There is nothing inherently wrong with being wherever you are in the social system; whatever judgments we have regarding the dignity of our work is a function of comparison. That is not to say that we ought to accept it blindly, as in the first stage, but rather to play the game happily and move toward people and experiences, rather than desiring escape. As Alain de Botton pointed out, we often forget that we take ourselves with us wherever we go and our anticipation for an escape is much more pleasant than its actuality.[7] In other words, if we are sad here, we will also be sad on an island somewhere. Finding meaning where we are—not complacency— can allow us to reclaim hope and our sense of wonder. Studies on expansive, creative experiences show us that these are accessible to anyone—you do not need to be an artist or athlete, as is the common idea.[8] For anyone, it is simply a restructuring of your own consciousness, setting clear tasks and dreams, almost like gamifying your own life. This stage is also transpersonal, meaning it goes beyond the individual self, toward others; toward tayo (together).

In Maslow's hierarchy, the one who is able to complete their needs becomes "self-actualized." This is the realization of our personal potential, both embodied and worldly.[9] This is not a static goal but a moving one, because once the individual satisfies their own needs, they can go beyond themselves, perhaps to help others attain their needs, or maybe to find themselves as part of the universal experience of being human, not limited by one's own ethnic biases. Maslow also pointed out that there are exemptions: One can attain the heights of self-actualization, although they have not satisfied all of their needs. That is because once we have reached the fourth stage, we see that our personal sense of achievement is no longer tied to societal expectations: We become who we can be. This is kapwa, applied to its fullest potential.

The Unburdened Companion

Echoing many ancient traditions, the aim of liberation from imposed systems (that is, the illusions of the world) is an attitude of play—not in the sense of manipulation, as in the second stage, but in the sense of being light and unburdened. In the Christian sense, it is of being kind and forgiving in a world filled with the potential for suffering and willful malice. The person who embodies this is called *magaan kasama,* literally a light, or unburdened, companion. These kinds of people may be people-pleasers masking their own difficulties. The true magaan kasama is charming and just very happy to be here. They embody the tayo mindset in that they would willingly participate in what is offered *(maki-sakay sa trip),* while still being able to recognize their ethical limits. This means riding along with conversational topics, activities, mood shifts, and so on. Riding along with others *(makisakay)* is different from letting others pull you everywhere *(magpatangay).* When they are tired, they say so; they are aware of their duties and priorities. They never whine or judge; they can be good listeners and great storytellers. Upon their departure, the others who enjoyed their presence are enriched, feeling as though they just enjoyed a good meal, *Ang sarap niyang kasama.* Sarap refers to being tasty, especially with good food, and it also has sexual connotations. But in this phrase, which can be literally translated to "Their presence was tasty," refers primarily to the pleasure of a good and satisfying meal. The magaan kasama simply embodies the values of kapwa, particularly pakikiramdam (social sensitivity) and *pakikisama* (camaraderie). They embrace the shifts of culture and personal identity; they become who they are, wherever they may be.

CHAPTER NINE

Reclaiming Values

There seems to be a notion that Filipino cultural values are "toxic." Here, toxic refers to imposed attitudes that hinder personal growth by trapping us in social expectations about behavior, personality, and attitude. We see that certain cultural values tend to suppress self-expression *(hiya)*, enforce conformity *(pakikisama)*, encourage a fatalistic mindset *(bahala na)*, and hold people to moral obligations for things they did not ask for *(utang na loob)*. The problem is that we tend to take these concepts out of their appropriate context in order to say, with a condescending colonial tone, that Filipinos live in a shame-based society that perpetuates passivity and harmful social relationships. Concepts are plucked out of native languages and applied to a foreign framework, so Western-oriented researchers tend to define them however they want.[1] Virgilio Enriquez called this tokenistic approach to cultural attitudes *"mala-pustisong gamit ng wika,"* which is using language like dentures. In other words, they are not your true teeth; you are just putting them on and pretending that they are. In any case, if it is true that Filipinos have a weak, submissive, and "toxic" personality, then they need moral empowerment to assert themselves better—or Filipinos need to be more individualistic.

Let us first ask the very obvious question that seems to be glossed over whenever we talk about "toxic" Filipino values: Why would we value something that is, as we say, toxic? If we assume that we are, deep down, stupid, then we do not have to ask this question at all, and we can move on to "empowering" Filipinos by teaching them the importance of ambition, self-esteem, and a competitive spirit. Alternatively, if we assume that Filipinos, as human beings, adapt to physical and social environments based on the best information they had at the time, then we can look at our ancestors, and each other, with much kinder eyes. It is not that Filipino values are toxic. It's that the systems in place—that is, our current environment—does not allow them to flourish. We live in a kaniya-kaniya world, where systems are often unintuitive because they were imposed by colonial rule and encouraged by generations of the Filipino ruling class—the *principalia,* and eventually, the burgis. These systems encourage ownership as a marker of status as well as competition for limited resources. So, in a world where "survival of the fittest" is actually "survival of the ruthless," strength is defined by domination and force.

But the truth is that we have survived as a society and as a species mainly through collaboration and cooperative resistance. Our history is one of subversion and bloodshed in the name of independence, not just against colonial powers but also against corrupt rulers. We survived through adaptation and assimilation. We have learned to share our success *(balato)* with our communities. Many of us have given up comfort for the comfort of our families back home. In coming together, we have built ties to each other, not just to remove oppressors, but more importantly to create systems that thrive on interdependence. When we know each other, it is easier to hold each other accountable. In small communities, even today, the corner store will lend goods to struggling households, to be repaid when they can afford to. I am not saying that this is the ideal system for every context. I am only saying that this system emerged throughout our history. It is the system that has allowed us to survive the horrors of war and foreign conquest and has allowed us to thrive in strange cities. But now that more and more of us are recognizing alternative ways of being, having been assimilated into systems that are foreign to our indigenous attitudes, the old attitudes can hinder growth. After all, they no longer work. In a system that rewards personal effort, why would I want to give to others who did not help me get where I am? Why should I feel indebted to them? In a system that commodifies individuals and assigns value to profitable personalities, why should I feel the need to suppress my personality? If I should expect any success, then I ought to be myself! But, again, this "self" is a curation, a product. The kaniya-kaniya system does not care about social relationships, except as far as they can be commodified: Relationships become transactional. We say, "I scratch your back, and you scratch mine." The successful are seen as intelligent, but this quality is only based on a norm that depends on access to resources, such as education and good nutrition. Furthermore, emotion is often removed from intelligence, which is odd, because if intelligence is our ability to adapt to the world by grasping its facts, then more intelligence should necessarily mean more empathy. After all, many facts about the reality of the world are intangible. So, to answer the question, we do not value toxic attitudes; we value attitudes that allow us to be resilient, reliable, and mutually accountable, which, unfortunately, are not useful in a kaniya-kaniya society.

Kapwa

It is important to remember that any useful interpretation of these cultural attitudes ought to consider kapwa in its core, as the trunk of an ancient tree whose branches imply multitudes and whose roots go deep into our shared ground of being.[2] *Kapwa* is often translated into English as "others," but this creates a distinction between people where there is none. Kapwa can be more appropriately understood as recognition of a shared identity or, as I like to say, an "us-ness." Kapwa might also be translated as "fellow," but this word merely implies a separate companion with whom one shares some similarities. Kapwa can indeed be used in this way, such as when a person refers to similarities directly: *"kapwa kong mahilig sa . . ."* (a fellow aficionado of . . .). But this is only one aspect of kapwa.

Virgilio Enriquez is the main proponent of the kapwa theory and a pioneer in the indigenization movement. Along with Carmen Santiago, they identified eight levels of social interaction, divided into two categories: *ibang tao* (outsider) and *hindi ibang tao* (one of us). These categories are not mutually exclusive; rather, they are on a continuum and are constantly negotiated.[3] While everyone is kapwa, we begin with the most general level of ibang tao, which is transactional and involves mere civility *(pakikitungo)*. Casual interactions *(pakikisalamuha)* can be invitations to participate in activities *(pakikilahok)* where it may be necessary to understand and follow the implicit codes of conduct *(pakikibagay)*. The threshold between ibang tao and hindi ibang tao is crossed when the outsider willingly joins the group, displaying internalized awareness of their social dynamics. This is called pakikisama, which is often translated as "conformity."

It is true that pakikisama can be weaponized to pressure people to participate in morally dubious or even criminal activities. An individual unwilling to embody the group's attitudes *(walang pakikisama)* is usually cut off from the social resources afforded by the group. There are, however, higher values that can neutralize the accusation of having no sense of pakikisama, such as *dangal* (dignity), especially in the fight for *kalayaan* (freedom), where subversion may be necessary. Nevertheless, pakikisama may be a form of initiation into a deeper relationship.

Building trust with others involves pakikipagpalagayang-loob (rapport). This means placing (lagay) your inner self (loob) before others, for them to see your most authentic self. Vulnerability is welcomed and honored. Having access to another person's truth means being involved in their life *(pakikisangkot)*. One must have the right assessment of the depth of one's relationship with others, otherwise pakikisangkot becomes an unwelcome intrusion. In this case, the intruder is often asked, *"Sino ka ba para sabihin ito?"* (Who are you to say this to me?) The deepest level of Kapwa is *pakikiisa* or sharing in oneness. This implies shared vision and passion. People who come together through pakikiisa share the struggle *(pakikibaka)*.

Negotiating the transition between ibang tao and hindi ibang tao involves pakikiramdam, which is feeling with another person. It is not simply "reading the room," which implies an active effort; pakikiramdam is an intuitive sense of other people's affect. It is social empathy. Through pakikiramdam, one knows if it is appropriate to joke, bring up a sensitive topic, or tease a friend. Relationships are valued, especially when they are hindi ibang tao, which makes it difficult to insist on one's preferences. When offended, someone may not want to cause any more tension, so they withdraw affection. This is called *tampo,* which is a form of sulking. Those with no pakikiramdam will find this frustrating, but those with it know that one must do *suyo,* which is an active form of affection toward a desired outcome, even if it is just to understand why a person is feeling tampo. Or, once the offense has been identified, one does *bawi,* which is an action that is meant to appease the one who is feeling tampo. *Bawi* means "to take back," and in this case, to take back an offense given. Spiritually, one also does bawi to offended spirits by offering something to them. This offering is called *atang.* To its extreme, pakikiramdam becomes kutob, a sense one has about things in general, such as the ulterior motives of others or even events (usually negative) that are likely to occur. If one has kutob, one can feel their environment too, as when one can sense things others cannot see, such as invisible entities. A person who is sensitive to these things is called *nakakaramdam* (one who senses things).

Pakikipagkapwa, the active relational form of Kapwa, can extend beyond social dynamics. Just as we treat people respectfully, we are careful not to offend nature spirits. This reflects an ecological awareness of the self as part of a larger world, comprised of unique elements, both visible and invisible, working together in harmony. In Filipino folk belief, an individual's well-being is dependent on their relationship with humans, spirits, and nature. This is the spiritual dimension of kapwa, a "kapwa ecology," if you will.

So, even when we weaponize the labels of these cultural attitudes to impose a kaniya-kaniya way of life (and this is when we call it "toxic"), we

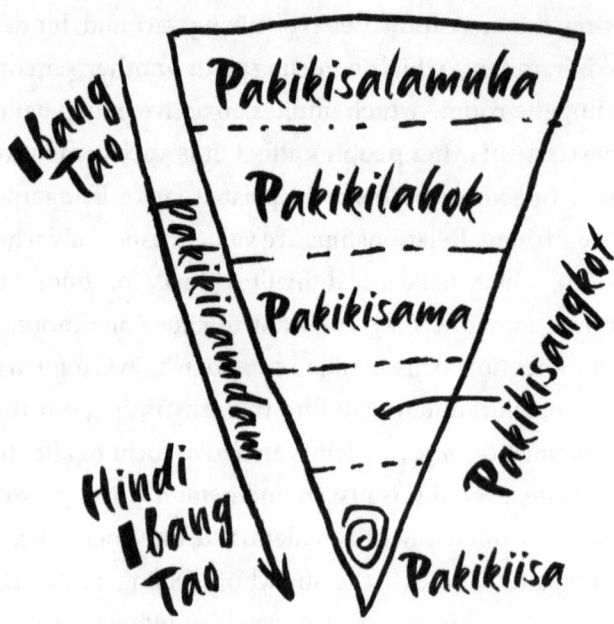

Figure 9.1. The levels of *Kapwa*

must challenge the imposition with this question: Does this lead me toward kapwa? Does this lead me toward other people or away from them, or even against them? If so, then we are only using valuable linguistic terms like dentures. We must reflect on what they truly mean to embody them appropriately. Let us now look at hiya and utang na loob and how they are meant to be interpreted in a kapwa-based orientation.[*]

Hiya

Hiya is usually translated as "shame," but practiced, it seems to refer more to the implicit expectation of acting with good manners. It is the inhibiting feeling that arises in situations where there is a need to maintain

---

[*] I have already talked about pakikisama above, and I will talk about bahala na in the next chapter.

a delicate social balance, usually between an individual and an authority figure.[4] A child might feel hiya when introduced to their distant relatives. They might not immediately play with other children; they might wait for others to lead. In general, one feels hiya when one is in a situation where they are not completely familiar with the customs of a group. For example, one might feel hiya when first introduced to a group. They may act timidly at first, masking their true selves just in case aspects of their personality are shunned by this particular group. One might also feel hiya when meeting someone for a first date, or when meeting someone they admire. Hiya is a form of social sensitivity closely related to the relational concepts of pakikiramdam and pakikisama. Here are the various qualities of hiya.

Firstly, it can only exist in the context of a relationship that a person values. If I do not care about a person, group, or situation, I will not feel hiya. There is nothing to maintain, nothing to keep, and nothing to gain, so it will be easy for me to destroy it or let it go. I will only feel hiya if I (even subconsciously) feel that there is potential in a particular situation.

Secondly, the first reaction to hiya may either be to freeze or flee, and a resolution to this is to say *"bahala na"* (Let it be) and carry on. For example, if a person is forced to display a talent in front of a large crowd, they might naturally feel hiya. It could be because they are afraid of embarrassing themselves. It could also be that they might ruin the well-crafted persona they created especially for that group. Also, it could be that they would not want to impose their talents onto others—not because they cannot do it, but because the focused attention on one person disturbs the dynamic of a shared engagement within a group setting. This momentary pause may cause social anxiety. The portal that leads beyond fear is bahala na.

Thirdly, guilt is not necessary to experience hiya. In other words, one might be more worried about the revelation than the truth itself. A person who did something wrong will feel hiya because their sins were revealed, not necessarily because they committed that sin. They might even feel that the person who revealed the truth is also at fault, and we say, *"Bakit mo ako pinahiya? Sana pinagsabihan mo na lang ako"* (Why did you embarrass me? You could have scolded me privately). Because the feeling of hiya is often experienced negatively, it can be hard to consider it important, or perhaps even ideal, in most social settings.

On the other hand, a person without hiya, called *walang hiya,* does not honor context-dependent social dynamics—they are careless about social expectations and insensitive about the feelings of others and thus are perceived as inconsiderate. As Jeremiah Lasquety-Reyes pointed out, if walang hiya refers to a lack of concern for the feelings and well-being of others, then hiya can be a morally desirable trait that can contribute to social cohesion.[5] Experiencing hiya and acting with hiya can come together, just as a person who is corrected for a mistake can feel embarrassed for being wrong yet take it gracefully without being defensive.

When hiya is weaponized, or imposed by others through statements like, *"Ano na lang sasabihin ng iba?"* (What will others say?), it speaks more about the insecurities of the one who enforces it than the person the statement was directed toward. Rather than supporting our kapwa, we inhibit their growth. We are not being *maka-kapwa* (for kapwa); we are being *maka-sarili* (self-centered).

Utang na Loob

Of all the concepts weaponized in Filipino psychology, utang na loob is, perhaps, the easiest to recognize. In the early days of social science research, utang na loob was interpreted by Charles Kaut as meaning a debt of gratitude in the same sense as the direct exchange of goods.[6] It can be seen, for example, in the expectation for children who have graduated to repay their parents after their parents paid for their childhood and education. It is the expectation of endless favors from someone just because you have invested in their success—somehow, you might feel entitled to whatever they receive. Some parents might feel entitled to anything their children achieve, even if they had little to do with it, and even if they have been incredibly unsupportive. If the child rightfully cuts them out of their life, the child would still be admonished: *"Magulang mo pa rin yan, wala ka bang utang na loob?"* (They are still your parent, have you no sense of gratitude?) The question then is: gratitude for what? The child did not choose to be born, but this is still the attitude of many of us when it comes to having children. We might ask a childless couple, *"Bakit wala pa kayong anak? Sino magaalaga sa inyo sa pagtanda mo?"* (Why do you not have any children? Who will take care of you in your later years?) Children become living investments that are expected to return with interest. They are expected to finish their education and, with their diploma, succeed in the world. From there, the duty of parenthood is seen as completed, and they can now reap the benefits of their years of hard work in raising their child.

Many parents expect to be morally compensated for their lost child-hoods spent in parenthood, for their sleepless nights spent caring for their child and sacrificing their own well-being and social life, for their strug-gle in navigating a corrupt system to ensure their child's happiness and future success, and for their very human attempts to guide their child's soul in the right direction. We can see that they hope that the child's utang na loob could be a form of solidarity with their family's past, with what they had to go through to give their child a comfortable life. That the child, who did not emerge from nowhere, would one day understand that they came from a historical context of personal struggle. Of course, parenthood is not for everyone, and, understandably, children ought not to be indebted to their parents, who gave birth out of their own free will, without their children's say in the matter. But we can see here that utang na loob is not just a transaction but a context. For those living in the kaniya-kaniya world, where self is prioritized over kin (and, more often than not, regardless of kin), utang na loob is an unnecessary tie to a strug-gling community, one that only keeps the hopeful individual tethered to a losing team. In this mindset, the weaponization of utang na loob is a debt *(utang)* one can never fully repay.

The thing is, we tend to look at utang na loob by itself, and rarely, if ever, in the context of kapwa, or even of loob. We have already discussed loob in the context of authenticity, and even then, we see how our interiority is a rich world of meaning. Why, then, do we talk about utang na loob as if it were a concept by itself, seeing utang without considering loob? Why would we have an inner debt? Could it be we have benefited greatly from the quiet efforts of all those around us, and many more who came before us? Could it be our existence, and continued flourishing, occur in the context of kapwa? As it is, devoid of context, utang na loob is indeed a transactional attitude. However, within context, utang na loob is a call to greater solidarity. It is a question of what we "owe" each other because we are all human.

Utang na loob is also used outside its most common weaponized form. When a person is in distress, they might cry out, *"Utang na loob, huwag mo akong saktan!"* (Please, I am begging you, do not hurt me!) This is a call to remember that we "owe" each other our shared humanity. We borrow from each other and share ourselves all the time. Utang na loob is a reminder of what we deserve as human beings, most especially dignity and respect. An exasperated and misunderstood person might also say, *"Utang na loob naman, hindi mo ba ako naiintindihan?"* (Oh, please, do you still not understand me?) Here, utang na loob becomes a call to give in *(pagbigyan)*, not in the sense of surrender or transaction, but in terms of allowing others to be limited, confused, misinformed, and ineloquent about their needs— just as most of us are, most of the time. So, while utang na loob—as well as many other Filipino values—can be, and are often, weaponized, their true value lies in contextual understanding as emerging from kapwa.

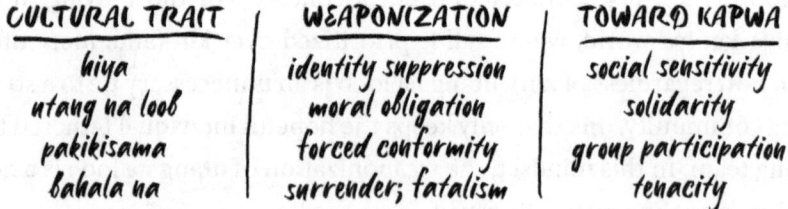

CULTURAL TRAIT	WEAPONIZATION	TOWARD KAPWA
hiya	identity suppression	social sensitivity
utang na loob	moral obligation	solidarity
pakikisama	forced conformity	group participation
bahala na	surrender; fatalism	tenacity

Figure 9.2. A quick guide to the weaponization of cultural attitudes.

Communication and Confrontation

The perception that Filipinos are "hospitable" is a strange thing to be proud of. On the one hand, it implies that we are gracious hosts; on the other hand, being a host implies having a guest, and historically speaking, our guests have also been invaders. Seen through a colonial lens, then, our supposed "hospitable" nature can be an affirmation of our submission to outsiders. Of course, we can see it from our perspective: We are so welcoming because we are a warm, happy people. Still, our hospitality tends to be a feature of the product that is the Philippines, as though it were a tropical resort for all kinds of tourists, and its natives are its willing and ready resort staff. Indeed, there are so many beautiful places to visit in the Philippines, and it is also very true that participating in the sunset crowd in a place like La Union, watching the sea of clouds from mountainous Sagada, or walking through historical towns can be a spiritual experience. It is also obvious that we tend to adjust ourselves to the preferences of visitors—this can be an extension of kapwa, but it can give outsiders the wrong impression. As I have been saying, we have only been looking at the surface of things, and rarely at what things are within. So, people see our beautiful attire, smiling faces, and hospitable attitude. They also see the outward manifestations of hiya, which they observe as timidity, or the outward manifestation of pakikisama, which they understand as conformity. All this is generalized to all Filipinos and subconsciously creates the pathetic image of a complacent and compliant native, only there to serve their master. Enriquez pointed out that these are only "surface values." They emerge from the same kapwa core as other values, but they are not the only values we have.[7]

We can see this in the way we communicate. Filipinos are often seen as indirect communicators, but that is only one mode of cultural communication. Our language is heavy with nuance, so, most times, we only need to know the context in order to understand a statement like, "*Na-ano mo na ba yung ano ni ano?*" (Have you ___ the ___ of ___?) Sometimes we might also use the filler word *kuwan,* a placeholder for things not immediately remembered. Melba Maggay identified various forms of indigenous communication.[8] Among them, we see varying degrees of expressiveness.

The *pahiwatig* or *parinig* is the most indirect, usually to express a hidden desire. It will most likely only work with people who are already close enough to each other to be aware of each other's needs. Tampo works great in this context, because it is something unsaid, yet it is also something the offended party wants the other to sense. An impatient lover might start hinting that they are already waiting for marriage during a very long engagement, by pointing to a picture or movie scene of a married couple and wistfully saying, *"Kailan kaya?"* (When will this happen to me?) They need not say anything else, and if their partner has any sense at all, they will recognize this as a sign. A child might also do parinig when they see their friend eating something delicious but are too hiya to ask directly for a piece because they might be perceived as *nanghihimasok* (entering without consent). So, they might say something like, *"Uy, ang sarap siguro niyan noh?"* (Hey, that looks really good.)*

If something needs to be said directly but direct contact is not an option, we might use an intermediary, who can act as neutral ground. This is called *pasabi*. A parent whose child will be visiting an estranged relative far away might ask them to relay an important message. This is also sometimes called *bilin*, something people leave for others, such as advice. A fighting couple might also do pasabi by asking a mutual friend to speak on their behalf. Note that this dynamic can work despite the accessibility of messaging applications. (And, on that note, if a person likes another person's post, this can sometimes be seen as a pahiwatig of some kind.)

A direct but respectful interaction is *pagtapat*, which is literally to face *(tapat)* something. *Tapat* also means "honest." A secret admirer

---

* I realized just now, as I write these silly English translations, that these statements are much more amusing in my native tongue, and I am sure that anyone who understands this context firsthand has surely heard these statements before.

might finally admit their love for someone by saying, *"May ipagtatapat sana ako sa iyo"* (I wish to tell you something). And, when they buckle, blush, stutter, and say, *"Ah, wala"* (Oh, nothing), their behavior is taken as a pahiwatig of the message they meant to deliver. One who is suspicious about another might confront them by asking, *"Ano, may ipagtatapat ka ba sa akin?"* (So, is there anything you wish to tell me?)

Toward the extreme end, a person who does not care about what relationship they might destroy might engage in *pangangalandakan*, spreading information without care, like scattering trash *(pagkalat)*. A person like this is often also seen as messy *(makalat)* and lacking in hiya (though not necessarily walang hiya). Social shame is definitely a threat in a culture that values interpersonal relationships, so this is a very confrontational attitude, even if one is revealing the truth. Connected to this is *paninira*, which is the willful destruction of another person's reputation by talking about them behind their back.

We see, then, that if a person is not initiated into the nuances of indigenous communication styles, they are more than likely to notice a few select kinds of communication. It is not just about the language being used; it is also about how the language is used, and how deep and meaningful a relationship is.

Confrontative Values

Aside from varying communication styles, Enriquez identified three confrontative values, to challenge the idea that Filipinos are only accommodating. These are bahala na (determination), lakas ng loob (guts or courage), and pakikibaka (cooperative resistance).[9] We do not just stop at certain values and do that for its own sake, such as doing pakikisama to be with others. If your motivation to go out and stand up for a cause is to be *seen* as doing so, then you are doing pakikisama for its own sake. Maybe you were pressured to participate in this cause even though it does not come from within you. It is therefore only cosplay. Pakikibaka, to share in the struggle, is an active manifestation of pakikiisa, or one-ness, the deepest and most meaningful level of kapwa. In the state of pakikiisa, we no longer see ourselves as individuals. We are part of this massive wave of humanity. Various thinkers during the Post-Martial Law era describe the same mystical experience of pakikiisa during the People Power Revolution, which ousted the Marcoses.* This peaceful revolution, driven by collective lakas ng loob, did not rely on military power. Faced with the tenacious prayers of the crowd, who walked arm-in-arm, the military forces did not know how to react. As Fernando Gonzaga pointed out, this revolution was spontaneous and deeply embodied, where cultural values were felt on a visceral level.[10]

This magic was attempted a few more times, again in 2001, which overthrew former president and action star Joseph Estrada (also known as Erap). Allegations of corruption drew people to Epifanio de los Santos Avenue (EDSA) once again, in what was called EDSA Dos. Although this protest was, like its predecessor, successful in peacefully removing some-one from a government, it was not as well-received, and Erap was eventually pardoned by his successor, Gloria Macapagal Arroyo, in October 2007.[11] And, perhaps I need not remind you, in 2022, the son of the ousted and exiled Ferdinand Marcos Sr., Ferdinand "Bongbong" Marcos Jr., was elected as the 17th president of the Philippines. Also in 2001, the same year people came together for EDSA Dos, was another protest, dubbed EDSA Tres, led by pro-Estrada loyalists who objected to his arrest.

Hopefully, being aware of these events in our recent history can bal-ance our tendency to romanticize the "ideal" Filipino—regardless of whether we see ourselves as hospitable or as confrontative. Despite our idealized kapwa orientation, we are still very human, existing in frail and

---

* Jaime Bulatao described it as an "altered state of consciousness" that was open to extra-sensory perception (*Phenomena and their Interpretation*, 1992); Virgilio Enriquez said that it was a valid reaction coming from our innate sense of pakikipagkapwa (*From Colonial to Liberation Psychology*, 1992); Mariel Francisco and Fe Maria Arriola saw it as a merging of divided society, coming together to herald a new age (*The History of the Burgis*, 1987).

illness-prone bodies, shaped by and trapped in unintuitive systems, often falling into comfortable kaniya-kaniya thinking. We must see clearly who we are and what we have been through while at the same time holding ourselves to the standard of what we could be. Only then can we hope for true inner and collective transformation, which is pagbabagong-loob (a change of the interior), or, as Enriquez called it, pagbabagong-dangal (a shift in dignity).

CHAPTER TEN

-

Revolution and Fate

Some might have started reading this book assuming the dangers of colonization and the liberatory potential of indigenization only apply to larger-scale, societal issues. But I hope it has become obvious that their basic processes can also operate on an individual level. We must not confuse the symbolic system—language, religious mythology, and so on—with the meanings they originally imply. Symbols are malleable and their meaning can be easily replaced, much like what had happened to the swastika, once a symbol of divine luck and prosperity, now globally recognized as a symbol of hatred and violence. That it represents prosperity is still held by those who use the swastika with spiritual intent. But there are many symbols of prosperity, each with their own contexts, and all potentially valid keys to unlock cosmic power. The concepts I have discussed in this book operate in the same way. Kapwa is not, by itself, meaningful unless it is appropriately applied in a prosocial manner, otherwise, if we let it get corrupted in a competitive, hierarchical system, it becomes just another "toxic" Filipino attitude. I have used these concepts broadly, to access human realities, and, frankly, this mindset is more akin to the art of poetry. In poetry, symbols are interconnected and placed in forms to access intuitive realities existing in a shared spiritual space that is both deep and vast. The indigenous concepts I have discussed in this book indicate an interconnected system. The individual is not separate

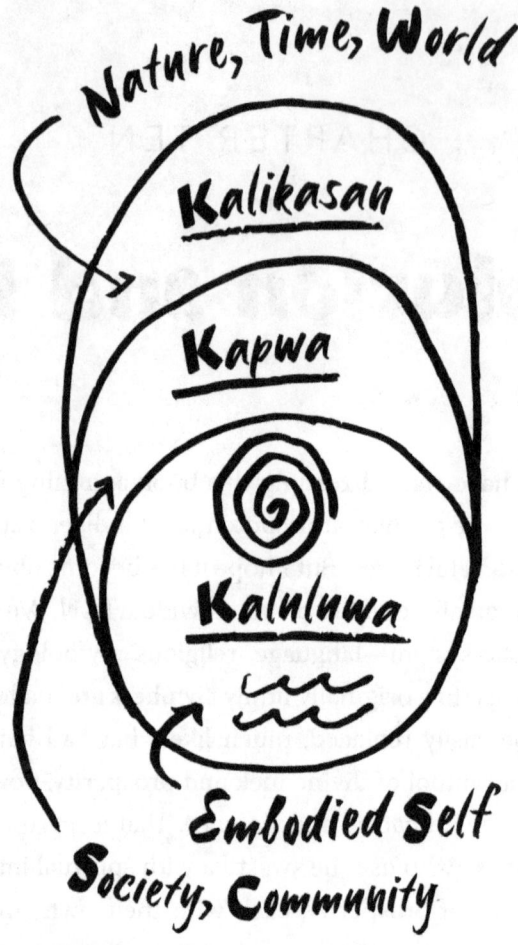

Figure 10.1. The three spheres of self: Kaluluwa
(soul), Kapwa (community), and Kalikasan (nature)

from the world but rather a fundamental part of it. Our existence implies
the existence of everything else—and it is also true the other way around.
We speak of "identity" as something distinct from the world, yet it cannot
exist without others to negate it, and in negation, our identity is affirmed—I
am because I know what I am not.

In my research on spiritual and paranormal phenomena in the
Philippines, I began to understand that our interaction with psychic

forces—spirits—is just an extension of our interaction with other people.[1] The process of socializing *(pakikipagkapwa-tao)* is applied beyond human relationships; it is also part of our relationship with the world. I have been developing this model for a while, figuring out the right terms to use, but underneath it all it is quite simply the notion of the self being distinguishable yet part of a larger field of existence.

The Scope and Boundaries of the Self

Our "self" (sarili) is shaped by our interaction with the world around us. There is no "me" without "you," as we define ourselves in relation to everything else. Everything that shapes who we are does not simply emerge from the individual body; we grew from a world that existed before us. Our bodies are also shaped through eons of biological adaptation, social pressures, and luck. We have survived, not mainly because of our ability to compete, but because we have learned how to collaborate with others and with nature. The greatest innovations of humankind have been manipulations of nature. The invention of the wheel, and then later the creation of more stable roads, allowed people to interact better. Today our communication is wireless, which is so much like magic: without knowing the actual science behind it, one marvels at how Wi-Fi and radio waves are used to transmit and broadcast messages, in real time, across the planet. One sits with nature, say in a garden or by the riverbank, and wonders how the hell we have developed chargeable scrying machines— and all manner of technological convenience—from the same earth that nourishes the plants.

The ancients knew the foundational ways of how we, as a species, learned how to manipulate nature for our own convenience, and they encoded this wisdom in myth and poetry. The entire universe is a natural flow pattern that moves from here to everywhere and back again. To name it is to confuse the name with what "it" actually is. Symbols have helped us manage our relationship with it. But each symbol works in relation to other symbols, and we tend to look at symbols as they are, rather than as an access point to a massive cosmic web. We know something is "up" because something is "down," "short" because of "long," "hard" because of "soft," "ugly" because of "beautiful." (This is an intentional simplification because "sloping upward" means something different than "straight up," and so on.) The point is this: To know one thing, we imply everything else. It is implied, for example, that to know "me" is to know everything else that is and is not me. Where, then, does sarili end? My skin? My clothes? My possessions? My preferences are defined by what I do not prefer. Even if I say that I like certain things, without much care for the other options, am I being intentionally ignorant of the truth that I have preferred one thing over another? Am I the choices I have made in life, and the choices I have yet to make? The people who I have loved and hated? All those alive today exist because they came from someone else's womb, who in turn came from someone else's—am I, then, an extension of my parents? Or are they simply an extension of my identity? What of my religious, educational, and social affiliations? If someone asked me who I am, I would answer with my own name or my family's (labels that I have been given at birth by someone else), or I would talk about where I graduated and what I do (which would say a lot about where I am affil- iated). Everywhere I look, there is the center of the universe. Everything emerges from all points. I am an extension of my parents, as they are an extension of myself: it is the same with my friends, with everyone else I have interacted with, and with everywhere I have existed. The word *sarili* implies ownership (for example, *sariling gamit,* my possessions) and agency (for example, *sariling pag-iisip,* independent thinking). It does not imply that all of these define me. At most, it implies that, for now, these indicate the cosmic point wherein I can be found.

Imagine, if you will, three concentric circles. All of it is sansinukob (universe). The smallest circle, sarili, is the self. It contains bait (sanity), loob (interiority), and alaala (memory), as discussed in a previous chap- ter. All three, these Thrones of the Holy Trinity, form *kaluluwa,* the soul. Kaluluwa is found within kapwa (shared identity), which includes relationships and social institutions. Kapwa is found within *kalikasan* (nature), which contains environments, nonhuman species, and other forces seemingly beyond our control. The boundaries that separate each one is called a diwa boundary—I use *diwa* to refer to conscious awareness or the apparent limits of one's consciousness. It is very possible to cross each diwa boundary, and it is frequently in those liminal spaces that we experience transformative crises, which I will discuss in a bit. When one is ready, the intentional process of crossing over involves pakikiramdam (feeling with) and pakikisama (going with). In this way, one transcends the kaluluwa level toward the kapwa level by being sensitive to social cues, going along with group activities, and being open to possibilities. The process of moving from the kapwa level to the kalikasan level is the same—we might even say we are practicing pakikipagkapwa (camaraderie) with nature itself. By being sensitive to the forces of nature, going along with its rhythms, and being open to serendipity, we find ourselves grounded in the primordial wisdom of the world.

You can try to see how this applies to you. Draw three concentric circles, and label them "kaluluwa," "kapwa," and "kalikasan." Within each area, indicate the various identities you assume. Within kaluluwa, include your personal preferences, significant childhood experiences, abilities, and so on—everything you feel defines who you are. Within kapwa, include your various affiliations and communities. What is your role in society? What do you do, and how does this impact others? Who do you know? Who are you in love with? Who are you in conflict with? Finally, within kalikasan, list the flora and fauna you have come to appreciate, as well as places of great significance to you (they can be human-made environments). What is your relationship with the larger world—with spaces and nonhuman objects and creatures? How do the spatial limitations of your daily environments influence your personal identity? How safe do you feel in the spaces you go to? How well do you know the paths of your every day?

This map of the self can be a guide for better understanding the next section. As you go through various crises of the self, try to see how they manifest in your own map.

Crises of Self

In Ken Wilber's attempt to unify the various schools of psychological thought, he observed that they all exist on a spectrum of consciousness. Each level has its own needs and so particular forms of psychotherapy can be applied depending on these needs.[2] On the Shadow level, the individual is alienated from themselves, discarding aspects of their being deemed "disgusting" or "inappropriate." On the Ego level, the individual finds themself split between "mind" and "body." Therapy on these levels involves facing unconscious forces. On the Existential level, the individual has aligned with their organic psychophysical self, and now faces the fundamental separation between the individual mind and the cosmic mind. Therapy on this level may involve more systemic or interpersonal approaches. In the sansinukob model, I ground these crises in cultural terms. These crises are not battles within the self; they are calls to realign. Our reaction to these crises is to go farther away *(lumayo)* or to come closer *(lumapit)*. There are six crises, each occurring within various levels of sansinukob, each carrying a learning potential. This should not imply a hierarchy or linear set of stages; we each face our own crises, and, for the wellness practitioner, it would be good to identify which one their client is going through, to provide appropriate support.

Within kaluluwa, we experience the first crisis: *ako* (me) versus *hindi-ako* (not-me). This is the battle between how we want to be perceived and what we do not want others to know about us. When we act in strange and unexpected ways, we say we are "not ourselves." This is the crisis of the Shadow. The Shadow, as it is discussed in Jungian psychology, is the aspect of the self that includes all that is ignored and suppressed in the creation of the ideal persona.[3] As part of social dynamics in Filipino culture, we can see this in *pagtitimpi* (holding in). Prioritizing kapwa can sometimes means biting one's tongue. To the extreme, this may lead to getting fed up, which we aptly call *hindi masikmura*, referring to the inability to "stomach" *(sikmura)* something. One will have to purge one-self, leading to the Shadow taking over, which we might call *nandilim ang paningin* (darkened vision) or *nilamon ng galit* (devoured by anger). These visceral metaphors show how embodied the experience can be. In many cases, the Filipino Shadow is shaped by shame and guilt, where personal values—especially one's dignity (dangal)—are pushed down or away. But one's truth will keep simmering within *(kumukulo sa loob)*, and when one can no longer take the heat, one tends to erupt *(pagsabog)*. This is one of the many important reasons why it is important to align one's inner self with one's outer world. The eruption of the Shadow—that is, the hindi-ako—is a result of one's denial of their own self. Working with the Shadow to encourage its unique creative potential is also the process of pagpapapakatotoo.

The next crisis occurs between katawan (body) and katauhan (self-hood). We can ask ourselves: Does my body accurately represent who I am? Do the perceived limitations of my body imply a lack within me? The dangers that occur when these first two crises are not properly faced may include self-loathing and guilt, and the potential splitting of the ego-self. We might begin to create fantasies of who we are that are no longer connected to reality. We might also see the phenomenon of *sapi* (spirit possession) as "entities" taking over to handle what one's waking consciousness could not. If these crises are handled appropriately, we can achieve self-understanding, and more importantly, self-acceptance. There is confidence in self-alignment.

Between kaluluwa and kapwa, is the crisis of *ako* versus *ikaw* (you). If we are unable to understand how connected we truly are, we might focus on our differences. We retreat into ourselves, and those who are like us, and we become suspicious of others. The next crisis would be *kami* (us) versus *kayo* (them). Systems are put into place to prioritize certain groups. Ironically, one's in-group identity is defined primarily by its contrast with an out-group. Warfare, in any form, strengthens differences, and when one group conquers another, neither has any identity to speak of. After all, there will be no contrast. It would be like trying to interpret white paint on a white canvas. These crises can thus lead to competition, exploitation, and oppression. Resolving this crisis requires enough clarity to embrace the coexistence of conflicting notions of shared identity and fundamental differences. Metaphorically speaking, we are all made of the same stuff, and, at the same time, to recognize myself, I must be able to recognize you as a being who is not myself. So, we learn empathy and begin to practice healthy social dynamics, similar to how leaves move with the wind. With enough care, we may experience the phenomenon of precognition that is culturally known as kutob, which is a sense that something, usually bad, is about to happen, usually to someone we care about. Perhaps kutob can also be a kind of hyper-empathy, since we can have it when we *feel like* someone is being deceitful or masking a tragedy. A lover might have kutob that their partner is having an affair; a parent might have kutob that their child is in trouble; a friend might have kutob that someone is going through a tough time despite their laughter. Kutob is a paranormal sense for things, but we must first care about them.

The next crises occur between kapwa and kalikasan, a conflict between tao (human) versus daigdig (world). The theme of separation continues here, where we see ourselves as distinct from the natural world, even though we grew from it, live in it, and survive through it. We hoard resources, breed living creatures for our meals, and consume without remorse. It is strange to see so many people store their resources only to wait for them to rot and then throw them away while many others die starving. We should hope that there is enough for everyone. It is possible that one does not have to starve just for another to eat. Maybe I eat the fish and the chicken in the same way my blood feeds the mosquito, in the way my corpse feeds the creatures of the earth, which in turn feeds the plants, who feed the animals, and so on. Ecological sustainability is the potential learning of this crisis. In folk belief, we already ask for permission from the spirits before crossing their territory—imagine them as kapwa who also call this earth their home. They live in forests and bathe in rivers. They lived in the land we built our houses on. The old man in the mound is called nuno, from *ninuno,* or ancestor. This folk belief may imply that, upon death, we return to nature—also that we are the descendants of nature. Once we fully realize this, we can look beyond the crisis of daigdig versus Diyos (God).

At this point, maybe, I have already done so much to work on various crises of illusory separation. I can integrate my conflicting selves (ako versus hindi-ako), embody my personality (katawan versus katauhan), empathize with others (ako versus ikaw), collaborate and participate in dialogue (kami versus kayo), and follow the rhythms of nature (tao versus daigdig). But I have reached the final crisis, the most glaring separation of all: that of the Creator and their creation. Daigdig versus Diyos. I have been told since childhood that I am not God. Of course, our conception of God is and has always been political, especially tied to our socioeconomic struggles. To be a "god" is to be handsome, wealthy, and renowned. But one cannot be a god in a world of contrasts because winning the game implies a host of losers: the deformed, poverty-stricken, and forgotten. We see suffering around us and think that no benevolent deity would ever want pain, sickness, and disaster. So, either God is so far away from our lived experience, or they do not exist at all, and everything is just apathetic randomness. Interesting that we only know what it is like to be healthy when sick—remember how you long for a spacious breath and a clear head whenever you come down with the flu. Grief and sorrow signify the absence of what had once been a source of magnificent joy and meaning. After all, we would not be affected by something we did not know about. Is it possible that God is not just in the mansions and champagne dinners and award shows? Maybe God is also in the least of our siblings: the hungry and thirsty, the naked, the sick and disabled, those deprived of liberty.* Maybe

---

* This is drawn from the parable of the sheep and the goats, in the gospel of Matthew, chapter 25, verses 31–46.

we forget that we are not just passive receivers and consumers in the world; maybe our care for them is God in action. What if all of it is God?

Imagine, then, with what limited metaphors we use to contain the divine, that the entirety of existence is a bubble. The air within the bubble is the same as the air outside it. We are inside the bubble and only recognize each other through contrast. Pain is as real as pleasure; success is as real as disappointment; love is as real as hatred and indifference. All of it—the air within and the air beyond—is God. Ancient Eastern traditions already understood this well. Filipino folk philosophy also understands it. I do not recall being asked whether I believed in a God. For us, it is not a matter of belief but of common knowledge. Spirits, serendipity, and supernatural mysteries are all too common in our everyday experiences. Unfortunately, "God," as we understand them, is the glorious King of Kings, sitting on his throne, hidden away in a walled fortress. Anyone who wants their blessing must bow; we are subjects in their court. God may be this king, also the man on the street. In world mythology, we commonly see gods disguising themselves as human beings, and many fall in love with mortals. Maybe that is the great mythic magic of love: to see God in another.

In summary, each crisis is moving away from or toward each other. Or, put in another way, a resistance to the dynamism of personality. Crises of kaluluwa involve holding on too tightly to who we think we are, while crises of kapwa involve holding on to what we are supposed to be as a collective, and crises of kalikasan involve hoarding things that are no one's property. To transcend these crises, one must learn to let go.

Letting Go

Ancient wisdom says that the desperate person will hold on to anything, even a blade—"*Ang taong gipit, sa patalim kumakapit.*" This can be interpreted as a call for violence, in that a person will do anything to protect their peace of mind. Alternatively, the saying suggests that one is holding on to something that can cut them. Either way, one can be wounded by their own desperation. Buddhist teachings recommend releasing desire and accepting the impermanence of the world. The Stoics taught the importance of accepting what cannot be changed, focusing only on what one can control. Jesus Christ said, in what may be my favorite biblical verse, to look at the birds, who eat without having to hoard their harvests. The Father feeds them—are we not also members of creation?[4]

Trust is difficult to do. On the one hand, one may be resigned to their fate, saying they would be taken care of anyway. This reminds me of the old story of Juan Tamad, who did not want to climb the tree to get fruit, so he lay down under the tree and opened his mouth, waiting for the fruit to fall, eventually. Something did fall into his mouth: the feces of a passing bird. Now, on the other hand, one might haphazardly risk their lives in the reckless pursuit of pleasure. They may end up hospitalized, in danger, or go into debt. Both characters may wonder if the universe was so provident, why they suffered, but neither truly trusted. Both these attitudes are closed off to possibility.

The word for fate, *kapalaran*, has within it the word *palad*, referring to the palm of one's hand. Maybe our fate, like palm lines, is already determined, and we can no longer do anything about it, or we have the power to take control of it, "taking the matter into our own hands." Both interpretations can coexist, especially in the popular saying, *"Nasa Diyos ang awa, pero nasa tao ang gawa."* This can be translated in many ways, such as "God helps those who help themselves" or "God has mercy on those who act." But this saying does not assure us of God's providence. It is just telling us that our efforts will be noticed, and maybe, rewarded—but we will have to do something about it. *Awa* also means "mercy" (or, in most cases, "pity"), so God here is not portrayed as a cold cosmic process that has equivalent reactions to every action—God is a merciful being. *God* simply refers to the projected sentience of chaotic uncertainty. Regardless of what we call this force, we assume that there is some order, some meaning beyond what we are currently aware of. We refer to it as a wheel, or *gulong ng palad*.

Sometimes we may be on top, and at other times we are crushed under its weight. The bottom is when we are *kapos-palad*, when we have nothing to show, despite our hard work. But we must trust that the wheel of fate should keep moving. If necessary, we must move it ourselves.

Regarding fate, we might also say, *"Kung para sa iyo, babalik at babalik din."* (If it is for you, it will keep coming back.) Lovers hold on to the hope they will end up with the one they are destined to be with. But it is not just a passive submission to chance. Romantic destiny is something we fight for. We must prove that we are worthy of our fate. One feeling regret over a lost lover will cry out, *"Bakit hindi mo ako pinaglaban?"* (Why did you not fight for me?) This wisdom goes beyond romance alone. We also fight for the dignity and comfort of our family, our children's futures, our creative passions and livelihood, and our strongly held convictions. We fight for our dangal and what we believe is rightfully ours, *pakikipagsapalaran*, which means "engaging with fate." We say this when we make any effort, such as applying for jobs, braving a terrifying situation, or competing for a prize. One trusts that things will happen the way they do, and that somehow, they might be rewarded for their efforts.

Bahala Na!

When we do not know what to do, we often say, "Bahala na!" This is an act of letting go of the anxiety of uncertainty. It is said that *bahala* comes from Bathala, the old creator god. It is odd and quite redundant, then, whenever we say, *"Bahala na si Lord,"* which means, "Let God handle it." *Bahala* might come from a Sanskrit word that means "load."[5] Bahala na then becomes "letting go of a burden." When we want others to take responsibility, we place it on them: *"Bahala ka na!"* (You deal with this!) When we want others to stop worrying about something we are willing to handle ourselves, we say, *"Ako na ang bahala."* (I will deal with this.) So, bahala na does not necessarily refer to any divinity in particular, but when it matches a spiritual worldview, it can imply trust in the divine.

Outsiders might only see the aspect of bahala na that implies a surrender, so it can easily be read simply as a resignation to fate, a kind of fatalism. However, experience shows us an element of determinism in this phrase, in that it is more often used to confront uncertainty creatively.[6] A student who spends sleepless nights studying is faced with a test for a subject they do not fully understand. A romantic has gathered enough courage to confess their affection for someone. Someone unemployed sends out their nth application letter. An actor or musician attends an audition. A writer submits their manuscript to a publisher. Someone wrongfully accused speaks up to clear their name. Advocates march the streets. The colonized stand up against the colonizer. In all these situations and more, we confront uncertainty. We say "Bahala na" and act, hoping to be noticed by a merciful God. The student may fail their exam; the romantic or job applicant or aspiring performer or writer may be rejected; the advocates may be shut down. We persist anyway. *Kung para sa iyo, babalik at babalik din.* The student may, after multiple tries, finally pass; the romantic might finally find the love they deserve; the job applicant might finally find the right industry; the performer might get the right exposure; the writer might, after multiple rejections, find an audience who understands; the advocates may start a revolution.

Toward Kapwa

The identity of the individual self is tied to and is largely defined by the world around them. We are not independent objects from nowhere; we emerge naturally from the cosmic processes that shape mountains, bend rivers, and encourage the flowers to bloom. Our personal and cultural traits are as natural as the sun's light and heat; we reflect each other in the same way the moon and the lake reflect the sun, and our (somewhat predictable) dynamism is as ordinary as the changing seasons. The sunset comes daily, but it is always unique; each person is a sunset, and at any point in time, the beauty of our deep humanity rarely goes unseen. History is not a line with a defined start and end, where we move from one place to another and never meet each other again—rather, it is a wheel with parts that occasionally meet the ground. We do not always know where we are going, but the wheel does not seem to touch the same area on this ground. We are all on the same trip.

In all of this, we have seen that, by our very existence, we are connected to all points of this conceivable universe, within and beyond the body. We are shaped by community, time, and relationships, and we also help shape the world: The choices we make become us, and it influences everything else. To exist and interact with people, systems, and environments is our participation in history, already. If given the opportunity, I would define what a human being is, at least on a psychological level, as self-conscious patterns, points of intersection in a massive web of meaning. By our very existence, we touch other lives and are touched by others too. We see this echoed in our ancient spiritualities, and regardless of how they manifest today, we can still feel the old spirits, the forms and forces that influence our everyday lives.

We must be careful about our tendency to prefer to exist in a constant state of healing. If we define ourselves by our historical traumas, we will not want them to be addressed and forgiven. If it gives us meaning, we may hold on to anything that continues to hurt us. But meaning can be derived from many different places, and I hope this book has expanded your own map. Our cultural identity is constantly in motion; all our lives are mythic journeys of initiation, discovery, and transformation. From our seafaring ancestors to the millions of overseas families today, we have found ourselves and each other wherever we are. But although we may be divided by vast oceans, it only takes a little bit of imagination to expand the notion of "archipelago" to refer to a global humanity—after all, underneath the tumultuous waves, even the most isolated islands are connected by the deep earth. If it was the kaniya-kaniya imagination that created divisions, boundaries, and classifications for the purpose of control and exploitation, then the antidote is a different way of thinking, toward the tayo perspective.

Today, hear the songs of the babaylan and enter a shamanic trance with the Christianized animist; visit the diwata of the mountains and the nuno of the mound; dance in modern worship feasts during the many colorful festivals across the archipelago; learn the meaning of the ethnic symbols in tattoos and woven patterns; and eat with others—remember what they say, that the best adobo is your mom's adobo. All this brings us back to who we are. This is the invitation of Sikodiwa. Just as the folk healer calls the wandering soul back to the body made sick by its absence, let this be our call: Come, return to kapwa.

Notes

CHAPTER 1
Indigenization

1 June Prill-Brett, "Voices from the Other Side: Impressions from some Igorot Participants in US Cultural Exhibitions in the Early 1900s," *Cordillera Review* 1, no. 1 (2009), 27–46, https://thecordillerareview .upb.edu.ph/wp-content/uploads/2021/06/3-TCR-I-1-Brett.pdf.

2 Reynaldo Clemeña Ileto, *Pasyon and Revolution: Popular Movements in the Philippines* (Quezon City: Ateneo de Manila University Press, 1979).

3 Mariel N. Francisco and Fe Maria C. Arriola, *The History of the Burgis* (1987; repr., Quezon City: Fuego y Hielo, 2019), 68–78.

4 Tom Sykes, *Imagining Manila: Literature, Empire, and Orientalism* (London: Bloomsbury Academic, 2021), 37–51.

5 Zeus A. Salazar, "The *Pantayo* Perspective as a Discourse Towards *Kabihasnan*," trans. Ramon Guillermo, *Southeast Asian Journal of Social Science* 28, no. 1 (2000), 123–52, www.jstor.org/stable/244 93002.

6 Nick Joaquin, *Culture and History* (Mandaluyong City: Anvil Publishing, 2004), 3–8.

7 Leonardo N. Mercado, *Applied Filipino Philosophy* (Tacloban City: Divine Word University Publications, 1977), 32–35.

8 Rogelia Pe-Pua and Elizabeth Protacio-Marcelino, "Sikolohiyang Pilipino (Filipino Psychology): A Legacy of Virgilio G. Enriquez," *Asian*

USD

Journal of Psychology 3, no. 1 (2000), 49–50, https://doi.org/10.1111 /1467-839x.00054.

9 Virgilio G. Enriquez, *Pagbabagong-Dangal: Indigenous Psychology & Cultural Empowerment* (Quezon City: Akademya ng Kultura at Sikolohiyang Pilipino, 1994), 3.

10 Ying-yi Hong, "A Dynamic Constructivist Approach to Culture: Moving from Describing Culture to Explaining Culture," in *Understanding Culture: Theory, Research, and Application,* ed. Robert S. Wyer, Chi-yue Chiu, and Ying-yi Hong (New York: Psychology Press, 2009), 4.

11 Zeus A. Salazar, "Four Filiations in Philippine Psychological Thought," in *Handbook of Filipino Psychology, Volume 1: Perspectives and Methodology,* ed. Rogelia Pe-Pua (Quezon City: University of the Philippines Press), 34–35.

12 Efren R. Abueg, "Filipino sa Konstitusyon: Iba't Ibang Pagbasa, Iba't Ibang Diskurso," in *Wika at Lipunan,* ed. Pamela C. Constantino and Monico M. Atienza (Quezon City: University of the Philippines Press, 1996), 164–66.

CHAPTER 2
Cultural Identity

1 Herminia Q. Meñez, "Encounters with Spirits: Mythology and the Ingkanto Syndrome in the Philippines," *Western Folklore* 37, no. 4 (October 1978), 249–65, https://doi.org/10.2307/1499205.

2 Jacob Rugare Mugumbate and Admire Chereni, "Now, the Theory of Ubuntu Has Its Space in Social Work," *African Journal of Social Work* 10, no. 1 (2020), v–xvii.

3 Aldous Huxley, *The Perennial Philosophy* (New York: Harper, 1945).

4 Albert E. Alejo, "Loob as Relational Interiority: A Contribution to the Philosophy of the Human Person," trans. Julia E. Riddle, *Social Transformations Journal of the Global South* 6, no. 1 (2018), 31–32, https://doi.org/10.13185/2799-015X.1088.

5 Alfred W. McCoy, "Baylan: Animist Religion and Philippine Peasant Ideology," *Philippine Quarterly of Culture and Society* 10, no. 3 (September 1982), 157, www.jstor.org/stable/29791761.

6 William Henry Scott, *Looking for the Prehispanic Filipino: And Other Essays in Philippine History* (Quezon City: New Day, 1992), 120.

7 Teresita B. Obusan, "The Mt. Banahaw Prayer: Amang Makapangyari-han," *Philippine Studies* 37, no. 1 (1989), 76–77, https://doi.org/10.13185/2244-1638.1218.

8 In particular, I draw inspiration from Demetrio's 1968 essay, "Creation Myths Among the Early Filipinos," as well as from *The Soul Book*, published in 1991, written by Francisco Demetrio, Gilda Cordero-Fernando, and Fernando N. Zialcita and beautifully illustrated by Robert B. Feleo; Eugenio's anthology of Philippine folk literature, the second edition of which was published in 2007; Jocano's 1969 monograph *Outline of Philippine Mythology;* and the second edition of the *Boxer Codex,* published by Vibal in 2022.

9 Leonardo N. Mercado, *The Filipino Mind* (Washington, DC: The Council for Research in Values and Philosophy, 1994).

10 Guillermo Q. Roman Jr., "TAO: Being and Becoming Human," *The Normal Lights* 5, no. 1 (2010), 81, https://doi.org/10.56278/tnl.v5i1.61.

11 Roberto E. Javier Jr., "Ang Tao sa Ka-Taw-An at sa Ka-Tau-Han: Pag-uugnay sa Pagpapakatao, Pakikipagkapuwa-tao, at Pagkatao [The Person in the Human Body: Being Human, Becoming a Human Person, Sharing the Self with 'Other' Selves]," *Malay* 30, no. 1 (2017), 70–85.

12 Virgilio G. Enriquez, "Indigenous Personality Theory," in *Handbook of Filipino Psychology, Vol. 2,* ed. Rogelia Pe-Pua, (Quezon City: University of the Philippines Press, 2019), 29.

13 Mercado, *Applied Filipino Philosophy,* 85–94.

14 Enriquez, *Pagbabagong-Dangal,* 20.

15 John N. Schumacher, "The Burgos Manifesto: The Authentic Text and its Genuine Author," *Philippine Studies* 54, no. 2 (2006), 293–96, https://doi.org/10.13185/2244-1638.1677.

16 Scott, *Looking for the Prehispanic Filipino*, 1–2.

17 Francisco Jayme Paolo M. Guiang, "Myth-Making and History Writing: Marcosian Revisionism as Evidence of Therapeutic Historiography," *Pingkian: Journal for Emancipatory and Anti-Imperialist Education* 7, no. 1 (2022), 23–48. www.scribd.com /document/617713884/GuiangFranciscoMyth-MakingandHistory -Writingvol7no12022.

CHAPTER 3
Cultural Dialogue

1 Farhad Dalal, "Jung: A Racist," *British Journal of Psychotherapy* 4, no. 3 (1988), 263, https://doi.org/10.1111/j.1752-0118.1988.tb01028.x.

2 Carl G. Jung, ed., *Man and His Symbols* (London: Aldus Books, 1964).

3 Jaime C. Bulatao, *Phenomena and Their Interpretation: Landmark Essays, 1957–1989* (Quezon City: Ateneo de Manila University Press, 1992), 22–31.

4 Ma. Crisanta Nelmida-Flores, "The *Folk* in Filipino Folk Christianity," *Banwaan* 1, no. 1 (2021), 14–16.

5 Francisco R. Demetrio, Gilda Cordero-Fernando, and Fernando N. Zialcita, *The Soul Book* (Quezon City: GCF Books, 1991), 9.

6 Alain de Botton, *Status Anxiety* (New York: Vintage International, 2004), vii–ix.

7 Gary Nunn, "Most World Maps Show North at the Top. But It Doesn't Have to Be That Way." ABC News, August 2, 2020, www.abc .net.au/news/2020-08-02/theres-no-such-thing-as-upside-down -world-map-racist/12495868.

8 Mark Epstein, "Varieties of Egolessness," in *Paths Beyond the Ego: The Transpersonal Vision,* ed. Roger Walsh and Frances Vaughan (New York: Tarcher/Penguin, 1993), 121–22.

9 Mercado, *Filipino Mind.*

10 Jeremiah Reyes, "*Loób* and *Kapwa*: An Introduction to a Filipino Virtue Ethics," *Asian Philosophy* 25, no. 2 (2015), 154, https://doi.org /10.1080/09552367.2015.1043173.

11 Jocelyn S. Martin, "The Vernacular as Method for Memory and Time: A Philological and Cultural Exploration of Filipino Concepts for Memory Studies," *Memory Studies* 13, no. 5 (2020), 836–37, https://doi.org/10.1177/1750698020944978.

12 Bulatao, *Phenomena*, 273–76.

13 Rogelia Pe-Pua, *Kros-Katutubong Perspektibo sa Metodolohiya: Ang Karanasan sa Pilipinas* (Quezon City: Pambansang Samahan sa Sikolohiyang Pilipino, 2005), 31.

14 Pe-Pua, *Kros-Katutubo*, 20–21.

CHAPTER 4
Learning and Unlearning

1 Stephen Baffour Adjei, "Conceptualizing Personhood, Agency, and Morality for African Psychology," *Theory and Psychology* 29, no. 4 (2019), 484–505, https://doi.org/10.1177/095935431985747.

2 Sylvia Estrada Claudio, "Has *Sikolohiyang Pilipino* (Filipino Psychology) Become *Sikolohiya ng mga Pilipino sa Pilipinas* (Psychology of Filipinos in the Philippines)?" in *Handbook of Filipino Psychology, Vol. 1*, ed. Rogelia Pe-Pua. (Quezon City: University of the Philippines Press, 2018), 240–42.

3 Salazar, "Four Filiations," 34.

4 Sykes, *Imagining Manila*, 1–18.

5 Zeus A. Salazar, "Ang Pantayong Pananaw Bilang Diskursong Pangkabihasnan," in Pe-Pua, *Handbook of Filipino Psychology, Vol. 1*, ed. Rogelia Pe-Pua. (Quezon City: University of the Philippines Press, 2018), 45.

6 Resil B. Mojares, *House of Memory: Essays* (Mandaluyong City: Anvil Publishing, 1997), 58.

7 Pe-Pua, *Kros-Katutubong Perspektibo*, 6–17.

8 Mihaly Csikszentmihalyi, *Flow: The Psychology of Optimal Experience* (New York: HarperCollins, 1990), 71–93.

9 Resil B. Mojares, *Interrogations in Philippine Cultural History* (Quezon City: Ateneo de Manila University Press, 2017), 3–18.

10 World Bank Group, "Philippines: Learning Poverty Brief," June 2022, https://documents.worldbank.org/curated/en/099000207152223103.

11 Renato Constantino, "The Mis-education of the Filipino," *Journal of Contemporary Asia* 1, no. 1 (1970), 35–36, https://doi.org/10.1080/00472337085390031.

12 Zacarian Sarao, "DepEd Confirms Receiving Proposal to Remove Marcos in 'Diktadurang Marcos,'" Inquirer.net, September 11, 2023, https://newsinfo.inquirer.net/1830123/deped-confirms-receiving-proposal-to-remove-marcos-in-diktadurang-marcos.

CHAPTER 5
Cultural Domination

1 Enriquez, *Pagbabagong-Dangal*.

2 Mercado, *Filipino Mind*.

3 Francisco Demetrio, "The Engkanto Belief: An Essay in Interpretation," *Philippine Studies* 17, no. 3 (1969), 598, https://doi.org/10.2307/1177781.

4 Jose Francisco C. Syquia, *Exorcism: Encounters with the Paranormal and the Occult* (Makati City: St. Pauls, 2006), 39–59.

5 Jose Francisco C. Syquia, *Catholic Handbook of Deliverance Prayers* (Makati City: St. Pauls, 2006), 251–55.

6 Syquia, *Catholic Handbook*, 109–10.

7 Enriquez, *Pagbabagong-Dangal*, 13.

8 Enriquez, *Pagbabagong-Dangal*, 11.

9 Laurence L. Delina, "Indigenous Environmental Defenders and the Legacy of Macli-ing Dulag: Anti-dam Dissent, Assassinations,

and Protests in the Making of the Philippine Energyscape," *Energy Research & Social Science* 65 (July 2020), 101463, https://doi.org /10.1016/j.erss.2020.101463.

10 Gaea Katreena Cabico, "Dumagat-Remontado Folk to UN: China Violated Human Rights in Kaliwa Dam Project," *PhilStar Global*, January 25, 2024, https://www.philstar.com/headlines/climate -and-environment/2024/01/25/2328444/dumagat-remontado -folk-un-china-violated-human-rights-kaliwa-dam-project.

11 Christian Ofalla Llait, "Tree Species Composition and Diversity in a Secondary Forest Along the Sierra Madre Mountain Range in Central Luzon, Philippines: Implications for the Conservation of Endemic, Native, and Threatened Plants," *Journal of Zoological and Botanical Gardens* 5, no. 1 (2024), 51–65, https://doi.org/10.3390/jzbg5010004.

12 Marcelino Q. Villafuerte II, Edna L. Juanillo, and Flaviana D. Hilario, "Climatic Insights on Academic Calendar Shift in the Philippines," *Philippine Journal of Science* 146, no. 3 (2017), 274, https://philjournal sci.dost.gov.ph/images/pdf/pjs_pdf/vol146no3/climatic_insight_on _academic_calendar_shift_in_the_Phils_.pdf.

13 Stephanie Sevillano, "Rapid School Calendar Shift to Affect Learners, Teachers: DepEd," Philippine News Agency, April 11, 2024, www .pna.gov.ph/articles/1222411.

14 Grace Nono, *Babaylan Sing Back: Philippine Shamans and Voice, Gender, and Place* (Quezon City: Ateneo de Manila University Press, 2023), 4–9.

15 Amierielle Anne Bulan, "'Malakas at Maganda' as Propaganda: Deceitful Art During Martial Law," *Nolisoli*, September 21, 2021, https://nolisoli.ph/49524/malakas-at-maganda-as-a-propaganda -deceitful-art-during-martial-law-abulan-20180921.

16 Mu Sochua, "Disinformation Poses a Grave Threat to Democracy in the Philippines," *The Diplomat*, May 4, 2022, https://thediplomat. com/2022/05/disinformation-poses-a-grave-threat-to-democracy -in-the-philippines.

17 Francisco and Arriola, *History of the Burgis*, 80.

18 Harvard Divinity School, "Corazon 'Cory' Aquino," accessed July 20, 2024, https://rpl.hds.harvard.edu/faq?page=8.

CHAPTER 6
Authenticity

1 Joaquin, *Culture and History*, 52–53.

2 Obusan, "The Mt. Banahaw Prayer," 78.

3 A. A. Phillips, "The Cultural Cringe," *Meanjin* 9, no. 4 (1950), 299–302, https://meanjin.com.au/essays/the-cultural-cringe-by -a-a-phillips.

4 Joaquin, *Culture and History*, 3–8.

5 Alejo, "Loob as Relational Interiority," 51.

6 Araceli Santos, "Loób," in *Vicassan's Pilipino-English Dictionary*, abridged edition, by Vito C. Santos, 240 (Anvil Publishing, 2006).

7 Rogelia Pe-Pua, "Unpacking the Concept of *Loob*: Towards Developing Culture-Inclusive Theories," in *Handbook of Filipino Psychology*, *Vol. 1*, ed. Rogelia Pe-Pua. (Quezon City: University of the Philippines Press, 2018), 382–94.

8 Leonardo N. Mercado, *Elements of Filipino Philosophy* (Tacloban City: Divine Word University Publications, 1974), 53–72.

9 Epi Fabonan III, "Dissecting Villar's 'Baliw sa Research' Statement," *One News*, October 14, 2019, www.onenews.ph/articles/dissecting -villar-s-baliw-sa-research-statement.

10 Felix Iglesias, "The Struggle to Save the Philippines' Architectural Heritage," *The Diplomat*, July 10, 2023, https://thediplomat.com/2023/07 /the-struggle-to-save-the-philippines-architectural-heritage.

11 Alejo, "Loob as Relational Interiority," 32–43.

12 Nikka G. Valenzuela, "Community Pantry: 'Not Charity, but Mutual Aid,'" Inquirer.net, April 18, 2021, https://newsinfo.inquirer .net/1420463/community-pantry-not-charity-but-mutual-aid.

13 Salazar, "*Pantayo* Perspective."

14 Mercado, *Applied Filipino Philosophy*, 85–93.

CHAPTER 7
Deep Spirituality

1 Julius J. Bautista, "An Archipelago Twice 'Discovered': The Santo Niño and the Discourse of Discovery," *Asian Studies Review* 29, no. 2 (June 2005), 191, https://doi.org/10.1080/10357820500221188.

2 Richard Humble, *The Explorers*, The Seafarers, vol. 3. (Time Life Books, 1978), 155.

3 Humble, *The Explorers*, 156.

4 Bautista, "An Archipelago Twice 'Discovered,'" 195.

5 Joaquin, *Culture and History*, 97–109.

6 Violeta Villaroman-Bautista, "Gamit at Etika ng Sikolohiyang Pangrelihiyon (Sinundan ng Talakayan ng Panel)," in *Handbook of Filipino Psychology, Vol. 2*, ed. Rogelia Pe-Pua. (Quezon City: University of the Philippines Press, 2019), 279–80.

7 Salazar, "Four Filiations," 37–38.

8 Christina Grof and Stanislav Grof, "Spiritual Emergency: The Understanding and Treatment of Transpersonal Crises," in Walsh and Vaughan, *Paths Beyond the Ego*, 137–44.

9 Francisco R. Demetrio, "Shamans, Witches, and Philippine Society," *Philippine Studies* 36, no. 3 (1988), 372–80, https://doi.org/10.13185/2244-1638.1329.

10 Nono, *Babaylan Sing Back*, 6–9.

11 Alan Watts, *Beyond Theology: The Art of Godmanship* (New York: Vintage, 1964; repr. New World Library, 2022), 175–77.

12 Alan Watts, *The Book on the Taboo Against Knowing Who You Are* (New York: Pantheon, 1966; repr. London: Souvenir Press, 2009), 14–16.

13 Watts, *Book on the Taboo*, 18.

CHAPTER 8
Personal Liberation

1 Abraham Maslow, "A Theory of Human Motivation," *Psychological Review* 50, no. 4 (1943), 370–96, https://doi.org/10.1037/h0054346.
2 Francisco and Arriola, *History of the Burgis,* 86–93.
3 Epictetus, *The Enchiridion,* trans. Thomas W. Higginson (New York: Liberal Arts Press, 1948), www.gutenberg.org/ebooks/45109.
4 De Botton, *Status Anxiety,* vii–ix.
5 Margaret Helen Urdabe, "The Tagasalo Personality," *Philippine Journal of Psychology* 34, no. 2 (2001), 59–62.
6 Thomas Szasz, "The Myth of Mental Illness," *American Psychologist* 15, no. 2 (1960), 113–18, https://doi.org/10.1037/h0046535.
7 Alain de Botton, *The Art of Travel* (New York: Patheon, 2002; repr. New York: First Vintage International, 2004), 5–26.
8 Csikszentmihalyi, *Flow,* 71–93.
9 Maslow, "Theory of Human Motivation," 382–83.

CHAPTER 9
Reclaiming Values

1 Virgilio G. Enriquez, *From Colonial to Liberation Psychology: The Philippine Experience* (University of the Philippines Press, 1992), 74.
2 Katrin de Guia, "Connected with All Life—The Enduring Filipino *Kapwa* Orientation, the Filipino Shared Self in a Postmodern Context," in *Handbook of Filipino Psychology, Vol. 1,* ed. Rogelia Pe-Pua. (Quezon City: University of the Philippines Press, 2018), 310–28.
3 Virgilio G. Enriquez, "*Kapwa:* A Core Concept in Filipino Social Psychology," in *Handbook of Filipino Psychology, Vol. 1,* ed. Rogelia Pe-Pua. (Quezon City: University of the Philippines Press, 2018), 287–92.
4 Jaime C. Bulatao, "Hiya," *Philippine Studies* 12, no. 3 (1964), 426–28, https://doi.org/10.13185/2244-1638.2659.

5 Jeremiah Lasquety-Reyes, "In Defense of *Hiya* as a Filipino Virtue," *Asian Philosophy* 26, no. 1 (2016), 66–78, https://doi.org/10.1080/09552367.2015.1136203.

6 Enriquez, *From Colonial to Liberation Psychology*, 82–84.

7 Enriquez, *From Colonial to Liberation Psychology*, 79–80.

8 Melba P. Maggay, "Mga Katutubong Pamamaraan ng Interpersonal na Komunikasyon," in *Handbook of Filipino Psychology, Vol. 2*, ed. Rogelia Pe-Pua. (Quezon City: University of the Philippines Press, 2019), 365–70.

9 Enriquez, *From Colonial to Liberation Psychology*, 86–95.

10 Fernando Gonzaga, "People Power as Immanent Collectivity: Re-imagining the Miracle of the 1986 EDSA Revolution as Divine Justice," *Kritika Kultura* 12 (2009), 109–27, https://doi.org/10.13185/1656-152x.1055.

11 Manny Mogato, "Former Philippine President Estrada Pardoned," Reuters, October 25, 2007, www.reuters.com/article/world/former-philippine-president-estrada-pardoned-idUSMNB00071.

CHAPTER 10
Revolution and Fate

1 Carl Lorenz Cervantes, "Philippine Parapsychology," *Explore* 20, no. 3 (2024), 414, https://doi.org/10.1016/j.explore.2023.10.006.

2 Ken Wilber, "Psychologia Perennis," *Journal of Transpersonal Psychology* 7, no. 2 (1975), 106–10, www.atpweb.org/jtparchive/trps-07-75-02-105.pdf.

3 Connie Zweig and Jeremiah Abrams, eds., *Meeting the Shadow: The Hidden Power of the Dark Side of Human Nature* (New York: Tarcher/Penguin, 1991), xvi–xxv.

4 Matthew 6:26–27.

5 Mercado, *Elements of Filipino Philosophy*, 183.

6 Enriquez, *From Colonial to Liberation Psychology*, 88–89.

Index

Bibliography

Abueg, Efren R. "Filipino sa Konstitusyon: Iba't Ibang Pagbasa, Iba't Ibang Diskurso." In *Wika at Lipunan,* eds. Pamela C. Constantino and Monico M. Atienza, 157–66. Quezon City: University of the Philippines Press, 1996.

Adjei, Stephen Baffour. "Conceptualizing Personhood, Agency, and Morality for African Psychology." *Theory and Psychology* 29, no. 4 (2019), 484–505. https://doi.org/10.1177/0959354319857547.

Alejo, Albert E. "Loob as Relational Interiority: A Contribution to the Philosophy of the Human Person." Translated by Julia E. Riddle. *Social Transformations Journal of the Global South* 6, no. 1 (2018), 29–53. https://doi.org/10.13185/2799-015X.1088.

Bautista, Julius J. "An Archipelago Twice 'Discovered': The Santo Niño and the Discourse of Discovery." *Asian Studies Review* 29, no. 2 (June 2005), 187–206. https://doi.org/10.1080/10357820500221188.

Boxer, Charles R. *Boxer Codex: A Modern Spanish Transcription and English Translation of Sixteenth-Century Exploration Accounts of East and Southeast Asia and the Pacific,* 2nd edition. Translated and edited by Isaac Donoso, María Luisa García Carlos Quirino, and Mauro García. Vibal, 2022.

Bulan, Amierielle Anne. "'Malakas at Maganda' as Propaganda: Deceitful Art During Martial Law." *Nolisoli,* September 21, 2021. https://nolisoli.ph/49524/malakas-at-maganda-as-a-propaganda-deceitful-art-during-martial-law-abulan-20180921.

Bulatao, Jaime C. "Hiya." *Philippine Studies* 12, no. 3 (1964): 424–38. https://doi.org/10.13185/2244-1638.2659.

Bulatao, Jaime C. *Phenomena and Their Interpretation: Landmark Essays 1957–1989.* Quezon City: Ateneo de Manila University Press, 1992.

Cabico, Gaea Katreena. "Dumagat-Remontado Folk to UN: China Violated Human Rights in Kaliwa Dam Project." *PhilStar Global,* January 25, 2024. https://www.philstar.com/headlines/climate-and-environment /2024/01/25/2328444/dumagat-remontado-folk-un-china-violated -human-rights-kaliwa-dam-project.

Cervantes, Carl Lorenz. "Philippine Parapsychology." *Explore* 20, no. 3 (2024), 411–16. https://doi.org/10.1016/j.explore.2023.10.006.

Claudio, Sylvia Estrada. "Has *Sikolohiyang Pilipino* (Filipino Psychology) Become *Sikolohiya ng mga Pilipino sa Pilipinas* (Psychology of Filipinos in the Philippines)?" *Handbook of Filipino Psychology Vol. 1,* edited by Rogelia Pe-Peu. Quezon City: University of the Philippines Press, 2018.

Constantino, Renato. "The Mis-education of the Filipino." *Journal of Contemporary Asia* 1, no. 1 (1970), 20–36. https://doi.org/10.1080 /00472337085390031.

Csikszentmihalyi, Mihaly. *Flow: The Psychology of Optimal Experience.* New York: HarperCollins, 1990.

Dalal, Farhad. "Jung: A Racist." *British Journal of Psychotherapy* 4, no. 3 (1988), 263–79. https://doi.org/10.1111/j.1752-0118.1988.tb01028.x.

De Botton, Alain. *The Art of Travel.* New York: Patheon, 2002. Reprinted New York: First Vintage International, 2004.

De Botton, Alain. *Status Anxiety.* New York: Vintage Books, 2004.

De Guia, Katrin. "Connected with All Life—The Enduring Filipino *Kapwa* Orientation, the Filipino Shared Self in a Postmodern Context." In *Handbook of Filipino Psychology, Vol. 1,* edited by Rogelia Pe-Pua. Quezon City: University of the Philippines Press, 2018, 310–28.

Delina, Laurence L. "Indigenous Environmental Defenders and the Legacy of Macli-ing Dulag: Anti-dam Dissent, Assassinations, and

Protests in the Making of the Philippine Energyscape." *Energy Research & Social Science* 65 (July 2020), 101463. https://doi.org/10.1016/j.erss.2020.101463.

Demetrio, Francisco. "Creation Myths Among the Early Filipinos." *Asian Folklore Studies* 27, no. 1 (1968), 41–79. https://doi.org/10.2307/1177800; https://asianethnology.org/article/1795/download.

Demetrio, Francisco. "The Engkanto Belief: An Essay in Interpretation." *Philippine Studies* 17, no. 3 (1969), 556–96. https://doi.org/10.2307/1177781.

Demetrio, Francisco R. "Shamans, Witches, and Philippine Society." *Philippine Studies* 36, no. 3 (1988), 372–80. https://doi.org/10.13185/2244-1638.1329.

Demetrio, Francisco R., Gilda Cordero-Fernando, and Fernando N. Zialcita. *The Soul Book.* Quezon City: GCF Books, 1991.

Enriquez, Virgilio G. *From Colonial to Liberation Psychology: The Philippine Experience.* Quezon City: University of the Philippines Press, 1992.

Enriquez, Virgilio G. "Indigenous Personality Theory." In *Handbook of Filipino Psychology, Vol. 2,* edited by Rogelia Pe-Pua. Quezon City: University of the Philippines Press, 2019, 29–42.

Enriquez, Virgilio G. "*Kapwa:* A Core Concept in Filipino Social Psychology." In *Handbook of Filipino Psychology, Vol. 1,* edited by Rogelia Pe-Pua. Quezon City: University of the Philippines Press, 2018, 287–92.

Enriquez, Virgilio G. *Pagbabagong-Dangal: Indigenous Psychology & Cultural Empowerment.* Quezon City: Akademya ng Kultura at Sikolohiyang Pilipino, 1994.

Epictetus. *The Enchiridion.* Translated by Thomas W. Higginson. New York: Liberal Arts Press, 1948. www.gutenberg.org/ebooks/45109.

Epstein, Mark. "Varieties of Egolessness." In Walsh and Vaughan, *Paths Beyond the Ego,* 121–23.

Eugenio, Damiana L., ed. *Philippine Folk Literature: An Anthology.* 2nd ed. University of the Philippines Press, 2007.

Fabonan, Epi, III. "Dissecting Villar's 'Baliw sa Research' Statement." *One News,* October 14, 2019. www.onenews.ph/articles/dissecting -villar-s-baliw-sa-research-statement.

Francisco, Mariel N., and Fe Maria C. Arriola. *The History of the Burgis.* 1987. Reprinted Quezon City: Fuego y Hielo, 2019.

Gonzaga, Fernando. "People Power as Immanent Collectivity: Re-imagining the Miracle of the 1986 EDSA Revolution as Divine Justice." *Kritika Kultura* 12 (2009), 109–27. https://doi.org/10.13185/1656 -152x.1055.

Grof, Christina, and Stanislav Grof. "Spiritual Emergency: The Understanding and Treatment of Transpersonal Crises." In Walsh and Vaughan, *Paths Beyond the Ego,* 137–44.

Guiang, Francisco Jayme Paolo M. "Myth-Making and History Writing: Marcosian Revisionism as Evidence of Therapeutic Historiography." *Pingkian: Journal for Emancipatory and Anti-Imperialist Education* 7, no. 1 (2022), 23–48, www.scribd.com/document/617713884/ GuiangFranciscoMyth-MakingandHistory-Writingvol7no12022.

Harvard Divinity School. "Corazon 'Cory' Aquino." Accessed July 20, 2024. https://rpl.hds.harvard.edu/faq?page=8.

Hong, Ying-yi. "A Dynamic Constructivist Approach to Culture: Moving from Describing Culture to Explaining Culture." In *Understanding Culture: Theory, Research, and Application,* edited by Robert S. Wyer, Chi-yue Chiu, and Ying-yi Hong, 3–23. New York: Psychology Press, 2009.

Humble, Richard. *The Explorers.* The Seafarers, vol. 3. Time-Life Books, 1978.

Huxley, Aldous. *The Perennial Philosophy.* New York: Harper, 1944.

Iglesias, Felix. "The Struggle to Save the Philippines' Architectural Heritage." *The Diplomat,* July 10, 2023. https://thediplomat.com/2023/07 /the-struggle-to-save-the-philippines-architectural-heritage.

Ileto, Reynaldo Clemeña. *Pasyon and Revolution: Popular Movements in the Philippines.* Quezon City: Ateneo de Manila University Press, 1979.

Javier, Roberto E., Jr. "Ang Tao sa Ka-Taw-An at sa Ka-Tau-Han: Pag-
uugnay sa Pagpapakatao, Pakikipagkapuwa-tao, at Pagkatao [The
Person in the Human Body: Being Human, Becoming a Human Person,
Sharing the Self with 'Other' Selves]." *Malay* 30, no. 1 (2017), 70–85.

Joaquin, Nick. *Culture and History.* Mandaluyong City: Anvil Publishing, 2004.

Jocano, F. Landa. *Outline of Philippine Mythology.* Centro Escolar University Research and Development Center, 1969.

Jung, Carl G., ed. *Man and His Symbols.* London: Aldus Books, 1964.

Lasquety-Reyes, Jeremiah. "In Defense of *Hiya* as a Filipino Virtue."
Asian Philosophy 26, no. 1 (2016), 66–78. https://doi.org/10.1080/09
552367.2015.1136203.

Llait, Christian Ofalla. "Tree Species Composition and Diversity in
a Secondary Forest Along the Sierra Madre Mountain Range in
Central Luzon, Philippines: Implications for the Conservation of
Endemic, Native, and Threatened Plants." *Journal of Zoological and
Botanical Gardens* 5, no. 1 (2024), 51–65. https://doi.org/10.3390
/jzbg5010004.

Maggay, Melba P. "Mga Katutubong Pamamaraan ng Interpersonal na
Komunikasyon." In *Handbook of Filipino Psychology, Vol. 2,* edited
by Rogelia Pe-Pua. Quezon City: University of the Philippines Press,
2019, 365–70.

Martin, Jocelyn S. "The Vernacular as Method for Memory and Time:
A Philological and Cultural Exploration of Filipino Concepts for
Memory Studies." *Memory Studies* 13, no. 5 (2020), 833–47. https://
doi.org/10.1177/1750698020944978.

Maslow, Abraham. "A Theory of Human Motivation." *Psychological
Review* 50, no. 4 (1943), 370–96. https://doi.org/10.1037/h0054346.

McCoy, Alfred W. "Baylan: Animist Religion and Philippine Peasant Ideology." *Philippine Quarterly of Culture and Society* 10, no. 3 (September 1982), 141–94. www.jstor.org/stable/29791761.

Meñez, Herminia Q. "Encounters with Spirits: Mythology and the
    Ingkanto Syndrome in the Philippines." *Western Folklore* 37, no. 4
    (October 1978), 249–65. https://doi.org/10.2307/1499205.

Mercado, Leonardo N. *Applied Filipino Philosophy.* Tacloban City:
    Divine Word University Publications, 1977.

Mercado, Leonardo N. *Elements of Filipino Philosophy.* Tacloban City:
    Divine Word University Publications, 1974.

Mercado, Leonardo N. *The Filipino Mind.* Washington, DC: The Coun-
    cil for Research in Values and Philosophy, 1994.

Mogato, Manny. "Former Philippine President Estrada Pardoned." Reu-
    ters, October 25, 2007. www.reuters.com/article/world/former
    -philippine-president-estrada-pardoned-idUSMNB00071.

Mojares, Resil B. *House of Memory: Essays.* Mandaluyong City: Anvil
    Publishing, 1997.

Mojares, Resil B. *Interrogations in Philippine Cultural History.* Quezon
    City: Ateneo de Manila University Press, 2017.

Mugumbate, Jacob Rugare, and Admire Chereni. "Now, the Theory
    of Ubuntu Has Its Space in Social Work." *African Journal of Social
    Work* 10, no. 1 (2020), v–xvii.

Nelmida-Flores, Ma. Crisanta. "The Folk in Filipino Folk Christianity."
    Banwaan 1, no. 1 (2021), 1–28.

Nono, Grace. *Babaylan Sing Back: Philippine Shamans and Voice, Gender,
    and Place.* Quezon City: Ateneo de Manila University Press, 2023.

Nunn, Gary. "Most World Maps Show North at the Top. But It Doesn't
    Have to Be That Way." ABC News, August 2, 2020. www.abc.net.au
    /news/2020-08-02/theres-no-such-thing-as-upside-down-world-map
    -racist/12495868.

Obusan, Teresita B. "The Mt. Banahaw Prayer: Amang Makapang-
    yarihan." *Philippine Studies* 37, no. 1 (1989), 71–80. https://doi.
    org/10.13185/2244-1638.1218.

Pe-Pua, Rogelia, ed. *Handbook of Filipino Psychology, Volume 1: Perspec-
    tives and Methodology.* Quezon City: University of the Philippines
    Press, 2018.

Pe-Pua, Rogelia, ed. *Handbook of Filipino Psychology, Volume 2: Application.* Quezon City: University of the Philippines Press, 2019.

Pe-Pua, Rogelia. *Kros-Katutubong Perspektibo sa Metodolohiya: Ang Karanasan sa Pilipinas.* Quezon City: Pambansang Samahan sa Sikolohiyang Pilipino, 2005.

Pe-Pua, Rogelia. "Unpacking the Concept of *Loob:* Towards Developing Culture-Inclusive Theories." In *Handbook of Filipino Psychology, Vol. 1,* edited by Rogelia Pe-Pua. Quezon City: University of the Philippines Press, 2018, 382–94.

Pe-Pua, Rogelia, and Elizabeth Protacio-Marcelino. "Sikolohiyang Pilipino (Filipino Psychology): A Legacy of Virgilio G. Enriquez." *Asian Journal of Psychology* 3, no. 1 (2000), 49–71. https://doi.org/10.1111/1467-839x.00054.

Phillips, A. A. "The Cultural Cringe." *Meanjin* 9, no. 4 (1950), 299–302. https://meanjin.com.au/essays/the-cultural-cringe-by-a-a-phillips.

Prill-Brett, June. "Voices from the Other Side: Impressions from Some Igorot Participants in US Cultural Exhibitions in the Early 1900s." *Cordillera Review* 1, no. 1 (2009), 27–46. https://thecordillerareview.upb.edu.ph/wp-content/uploads/2021/06/3-TCR-I-1-Brett.pdf.

Reyes, Jeremiah. "*Loób* and *Kapwa:* An Introduction to a Filipino Virtue Ethics." *Asian Philosophy* 25, no. 2 (2015), 148–71. https://doi.org/10.1080/09552367.2015.1043173.

Roman, Guillermo Q., Jr. "TAO: Being and Becoming Human." *The Normal Lights* 5, no. 1 (2010), 77–94. https://doi.org/10.56278/tnl.v5i1.61.

Sabino, Melencio T. *Karunungan ng Dios.* 1955. www.scribd.com/document/341972839/Karunungan-Ng-Diyos-1955-Melencio-Sabino.

Salazar, Zeus A. "Ang Pantayong Pananaw Bilang Diskursong Pangkabihasnan." In *Handbook of Filipino Psychology, Vol. 1,* edited by Rogelia Pe-Pua. Quezon City: University of the Philippines Press, 2018, 43–61.

Salazar, Zeus A. "Four Filiations in Philippine Psychological Thought." In *Handbook of Filipino Psychology, Vol. 1,* edited by Rogelia Pe-Pua. Quezon City: University of the Philippines Press, 2018, 32–42.

Salazar, Zeus A. "The *Pantayo* Perspective as a Discourse Towards *Kabi-hasnan*." Translated by Ramon Guillermo. *Southeast Asian Journal of Social Science* 28, no. 1 (2000), 123–52. www.jstor.org/stable/24493002.

Santos, Araceli. "Loób." In *Vicassan's Pilipino-English Dictionary,* abridged edition, by Vito C. Santos. Anvil Publishing. 2019.

Sarao, Zacarian. "DepEd Confirms Receiving Proposal to Remove Marcos in 'Diktadurang Marcos.'" Inquirer.net, September 11, 2023. https://newsinfo.inquirer.net/1830123/deped-confirms-receiving-proposal-to-remove-marcos-in-diktadurang-marcos.

Schumacher, John N. "The Burgos Manifesto: The Authentic Text and Its Genuine Author." *Philippine Studies* 54, no. 2 (2006), 153–304. https://doi.org/10.13185/2244-1638.1677.

Scott, William Henry. *Looking for the Prehispanic Filipino: And Other Essays in Philippine History.* Quezon City: New Day, 1992.

Sevillano, Stephanie. "Rapid School Calendar Shift to Affect Learners, Teachers: DepEd." Philippine News Agency, April 11, 2024. www.pna.gov.ph/articles/1222411.

Sochua, Mu. "Disinformation Poses a Grave Threat to Democracy in the Philippines." *The Diplomat,* May 4, 2022. https://thediplomat.com/2022/05/disinformation-poses-a-grave-threat-to-democracy-in-the-philippines.

Sykes, Tom. *Imagining Manila: Literature, Empire, and Orientalism.* London: Bloomsbury Academic, 2021.

Syquia, Jose Francisco C. *Catholic Handbook of Deliverance Prayers.* Makati City: St. Pauls, 2006.

Syquia, Jose Francisco C. *Exorcism: Encounters with the Paranormal and the Occult.* Makati City: St. Pauls, 2006.

Szasz, Thomas. "The Myth of Mental Illness." *American Psychologist* 15, no. 2 (1960), 113–18. https://doi.org/10.1037/h0046535.

Urdabe, Margaret Helen. "The Tagasalo Personality." *Philippine Journal of Psychology* 34, no. 2 (2001), 45–65.

Valenzuela, Nikka G. "Community Pantry: 'Not Charity, but Mutual Aid.'" Inquirer.net, April 18, 2021. https://newsinfo.inquirer.net/1420463/community-pantry-not-charity-but-mutual-aid.

Villafuerte, Marcelino Q. II, Edna L. Juanillo, and Flaviana D. Hilario. "Climatic Insights on Academic Calendar Shift in the Philippines." *Philippine Journal of Science* 146, no. 3 (2017), 267–76. https://phil journalsci.dost.gov.ph/images/pdf/pjs_pdf/vol146no3/climatic _insight_on_academic_calendar_shift_in_the_Phils_.pdf.

Villaroman-Bautista, Violeta. "Gamit at Etika ng Sikolohiyang Pangre-lihiyon (Sinundan ng Talakayan ng Panel)." In *Handbook of Filipino Psychology, Vol. 1,* edited by Rogelia Pe-Pua. Quezon City: University of the Philippines Press, 2018, 273–84.

Walsh, Roger, and Frances Vaughan, eds. *Paths Beyond the Ego: The Transpersonal Vision.* New York: Tarcher/Penguin, 1993.

Watts, Alan. *Beyond Theology: The Art of Godmanship.* New York: Vintage, 1964. Reprinted New World Library, 2022.

Watts, Alan. *The Book on the Taboo Against Knowing Who You Are.* New York: Pantheon, 1966. Reprinted London: Souvenir Press, 2009.

Wilber, Ken. "Psychologia Perennis." *Journal of Transpersonal Psychology* 7, no. 2 (1975), 106–10. www.atpweb.org/jtparchive/trps-07-75-02-105.pdf.

World Bank Group. "Philippines: Learning Poverty Brief." June 2022. https://documents.worldbank.org/curated/en/099000207152223103.

Zweig, Connie, and Jeremiah Abrams, eds. *Meeting the Shadow: The Hidden Power of the Dark Side of Human Nature.* New York: Tarcher/Penguin, 1991.

About the Author

Photo by Carl Lorenz Cervantes

Carl Lorenz Cervantes is a psychologist and researcher. Cervantes holds a master's degree in counseling psychology from Ateneo de Manila University and is currently a senior lecturer at the University of the Philippines in Diliman, Quezon City. He runs an Instagram, @sikodiwa, where he shares posts about topics such as climate issues, healing, and social responsibility through the lens of Filipino psychology. Cervantes also runs a Substack illuminating Filipino culture, Indigenous practices, spirituality, religion, and psychology.

About North Atlantic Books

North Atlantic Books (NAB) is an independent, nonprofit publisher committed to a bold exploration of the relationships between mind, body, spirit, and nature. Founded in 1974, NAB aims to nurture a holistic view of the arts, sciences, humanities, and healing. To make a donation or to learn more about our books, authors, events, and newsletter, please visit www.northatlanticbooks.com.